The Key Teacher in School

THE ATTACHMENT AWARE SCHOOL SERIES
Bridging the gap for troubled pupils

Other books in the
Attachment Aware Schools Collection®

ATTACHMENT AWARE SCHOOLS COLLECTION®

ATTACHMENT AWARE SCHOOL SERIES

Bridging the gap for troubled pupils

Book 3

The Key Teacher in School

Louise Michelle Bombèr

Worth Publishing

First published 2016 by Worth Publishing Ltd
worthpublishing.com

Printed and bound by CPI Group (UK) Ltd., Croydon CR0 4YY

British Library Cataloguing in Publication Data
A catalogue record for this book is available from the British Library
ISBN   9781903269299

Cover and text design by Anna Murphy

For Jane Airey,
who played a significant role
in my journey

Biography

Louise Michelle Bombèr is a specialist Attachment Lead Teacher and a therapist. She has worked for many years with children and young people who have experienced significant relational traumas and losses. Working in many different contexts she is passionate about ensuring these pupils have opportunity to adapt and recover so that they can make the most of all that school offers. She continues to work as a practitioner using Theraplay®, PACE, DDP and sensory interventions to support children and their parents.

Louise is the author of *Inside I'm Hurting*, *What About Me?*, co-author with Dr Dan Hughes of *Settling to Learn* and contributor to *Teenagers and Attachment*. Her work has been greatly influenced by John Bowlby, Dan Hughes, Daniel Siegel, Bruce Perry and Gabor Maté. Louise advises, trains and supports education professionals and families, and is involved in direct work with children and young people in class, in the therapy room and at an allotment project, PLOT 22 (*and see* touchbase.org.uk). She heads up a network which enables Attachment Leads to be trained to provide advocacy and support in individual schools across the UK (attachmentleadnetwork.net).

Acknowledgements

Thanks to Dr Kim Golding for her continued partnership with me, and my long standing supervisor Penny Auton, who has walked alongside me in my professional journey over many, many years. I would like to thank Jenny Peters in the UK and Glen Cooper in the USA for generously providing me with commentary on Circle of Security®, which is such an invaluable resource to all those wanting to make a difference in children's lives.

I would like to honour all those parents and carers that have shared their stories so vulnerably with me over the years as to what it is like to parent these children. I admire you and so wish that your children could see what I see, how much you deeply love them and root for them and how you desire for them to know how much they are valued, special and that they 'belong' to your family. This is so hard for them to take in.

My current TouchBase™ team - Jennie Fellows, Julia Wilde, Keeley de Freese, Becs Uvieghara, Natalie Miller, Tania Druce,

The Key Teacher in School

Alice Mallorie and Henrietta Kuhudzai for your dedication
and commitment to these children; it doesn't go unnoticed.
My national trainers, Anne Henderson, Clare Langhorne,
Alison Lumley, Helen Wallace and Helen Wright who so
passionately deliver materials they believe in, whilst continuing as
practitioners actively involved with many pupils. All the support
assistants and mentors with whom I have journeyed since 2000;
together we have learned what is needed.

My editor and friend Andrea Perry who encourages
and mobilises me into further creativity. My husband
Jonathan Fordham, who often releases me from household
responsibilities because he believes in this cause as much as I
do. Thanks for holding the fort when I bury my head in books
and my laptop! Lucinda and Steve Smith who lead with both
gentleness and strength, continuing to be really behind my vision
to see dignity restored. Nothing goes unnoticed.

All the brave families who have endured more than many
will ever know and yet remain standing clothed in dignity and
strength and armed with fierce compassion for their hurting
children. May this series of books play some part in raising much
needed awareness so that you can take a step back, trusting
the schools your children attend to nurture them into all they
should have been first time around.

Foreword

This guide for the Key Teacher is an important addition to the **Attachment Aware School Series**. Louise clearly articulates the importance of all members of Team Pupil in helping developmentally traumatised children thrive as a result of their time in school. Here the Key Teacher will gain important guidance about how to work as part of the team, fulfilling her particular role in helping pupils learn.

In the late 1800's a little girl of 19 months called Helen Keller became ill. She lost the ability to see and hear. Her story has been an inspiration to many. My purpose in mentioning it is to draw attention to two parts of this story relevant to the messages Louise gives us.

Firstly, the impact of the devastating loss of sight and hearing upon the small child. Helen is cut off from the world. She is described, in biographies*, as becoming wild and unruly. In reading this description I was reminded of developmentally traumatised pupils, whose own fear, anger and anxiety can lead to social isolation and challenging behaviour.

Secondly, the role of her teacher, Anne Sullivan, in reconnecting Helen back to the world: for Helen's story is ultimately one of disconnection and connection. Illness robbed Helen of her primary means of connection, just as surely as developmental trauma robs our pupils of the same. Her Key Teacher found a way to give Helen her connection back. Without that relationship, Helen's educational achievements are unlikely to have happened.

This is the message of Louise's book. To be successful, the Key Teacher works, as part of Team Pupil, to connect her pupils to the social world, and ultimately to learning. This is a challenging task because, unlike Helen Keller, developmentally traumatised pupils fear this connection. They resist the thing that has hurt them so much in the past. Though connection, however, the Key Teacher can fulfil her responsibilities to teach, guide, discover and fulfil the potential of the pupils who come to school with such disadvantage.

> When we do the best that we can, we never know what miracle is wrought in our life, or in the life of another.
>
> Helen Keller**

Louise sets the challenge to Key Teachers to become inspirational leaders. In *The Key Teacher in School*, she provides a road map for fulfilling this task. Team Pupil helps children to experience safety in connection; the Key Teacher can build on this connection to truly help pupils fulfil their potential.

Kim S Golding, 2016

*   *biography.com/people/helen-keller-9361967 (accessed 31st May 2016)*

** *brainyquote.com/quotes/quotes/h/helenkelle124456.html (accessed 31st May 2016)*

The Key Teacher in School

Please note: In this book I reference material from my earlier publications, using acronyms for their titles for accessibility. These books form a key resource for developing attachment awareness and trauma informed interventions in schools, and provide background reading for the **Attachment Aware School Series.**

Contents

continues/...

Introduction

This pocket-sized book is part of the **Attachment Aware School Series**. The series has come about in response to an increasing understanding that security, through the experience of secure relationships, is necessary for every child to be able to settle to learn and make the most of all the educational opportunities out there. It is only when a child's **attachment system** is attended to that their **exploratory system** can really come into play.

Some children may have learned security outside school through their experience of relationships to date - others may not. Some pupils find settling into learning incredibly difficult, especially those who have a history of not being attended to, or responded to sufficiently, or often enough; of neglect, traumatic experience or significant loss. If circumstances have ruptured or inhibited the development of an internal, felt sense of security, then children often experience huge anxiety - sometimes unnoted by those of us observing.

The Key Teacher in School

These pupils are not in a position to learn or take up the huge range of opportunities available to them in school YET. So in school, we must first address their need for security and stability - by providing them with a consistent, reliable, empathic, attuned attachment relationship in school. Only then can we expect them to make progress with learning, and to fully engage with school life.

On really difficult days, even the most securely attached child - or adult - may find learning a struggle. So this series of pocket books endorses the view that if a school is fully attachment aware, and indeed, trauma informed, *all children and staff will benefit*. Ideally all staff will have attachment aware training as their foundation, and with this background will appreciate that for some pupils a specific, targeted relational intervention will be a life-line.

In the **Attachment Aware School Series** we'll advocate having a small tight team around these specific pupils. So, in school we will have Team Lee, Team Grace, Team Aiden - Team Pupil: four or five people in different positions of responsibility in the school. All believing *in* and rooting *for* the pupil.

> Having several good attachment relationships predicts better self-control, behaviour and relationships.
>
> Belsky et al 2007

In the primary phase, this team will usually be made up of the Key Adult, a back-up adult if appropriate, the class teacher, and a Senior Manager (SENCO or INCO, the Assistant Head or the Head). In the secondary phase, this would usually be the Key Adult, the form tutor, a subject teacher (*see* p.27), and one or two Senior Managers (the Head of Year, the SENCO/INCO and the Assistant Head). In addition to this school-based team, each pupil needs to know that their parents or carers are on board in their education, trusting those involved to support their child and actively working in tight partnership within their unique Team.

With this in mind, there are five books in the **Attachment Aware School Series**, each reflecting the different roles of the different individuals in the Team around the pupil (one pocket book for each member of the Team). The series is written to help this valuable community work well together and hold the pupil in mind, shoring the pupil up when necessary, serving as an anchor so that anxieties can be relieved; freeing up the possibility for this child or young person to become all they were intended to become, first time around. I have also included a pocket book for the parents or carers of the child or young person, since they will be and often are valuable contributors to the school Team.

Throughout each book you'll find some key terms are highlighted in **bold**: you'll find all of these in the **Glossary** on p.95.

3

The Key Teacher in School

This particular book is intended for those who have been identified as the classroom teachers, subject teachers, individual support teachers, nurture group teachers, tutors and form tutors who, as **Key Teachers** and part of Team Pupil, will lead the way in terms of how learning is presented for a particular troubled pupil.

These **Key Teachers** have a significant role in Team Pupil as inspirational leaders either in general learning or a particular subject area. They can hold the focus on the pupil's areas of strength and gifts, as well as modelling a passion for learning. **Key Teachers** spot opportunities to extend the pupil's **exploratory system** (*see* p.99) so that the pupil can begin to take the risks required in learning, and then discover how energising and liberating doing so can be.

In the primary phase, a **Key Teacher** chosen for Team Pupil could be the main class teacher, the nurture group teacher or the teacher who spends the majority of their time with the pupil. In the secondary phase, teachers identified for a key role could be the form tutor *and* a teacher who specialises in the area in which the pupil has a strength and/or interest (to help boost their resilience). The pupils I've worked with have had art, drama and P.E. teachers taking on this role in the main, but the most important factor is that the pupil can identify with them. The team can include one or two **Key Teachers** as appropriate. Every Team Pupil will look different, as every pupil is different.

So, if you've been asked to play a part in Team Pupil, you can consider this a real honour, as you have been identified as someone who could make a big difference in the life of a child or young person. You may have been noticed as having a lovely manner with the pupils in your care. You may have been observed engaging in a meaningful way or maybe unlocking their gifts by how you relate to them and teach. You may have been described by the pupil themselves as a 'good teacher' or someone who 'understands' them. In the therapy context I usually hear comments such as *"They get me"*, *"They're nice"*, *"They're not like all the others"*, *"They notice"*, *"They make me laugh"*. When I hear these kinds of statements from the pupils themselves I know there is hope! Everyone needs at least one person on their side cheering them on towards the finishing line. This is such rewarding and valuable work. Not only will the pupils benefit from having you in Team Pupil, but you'll benefit too, however long it takes to feel that.

Teachers are well respected professionals who have significant responsibility for the whole class or classes. Schools have grown considerably over the last ten years, and so has the number of pupils each teacher is responsible for. So at the beginning of a book like this it is important to state that all teachers need to be protected to teach. This is their core work within school. At the same time, I hope this book will inspire you to be the best teacher you can be, relating to the pupils who are the hardest to reach, working to engage their interest in learning, within your role in Team Pupil. The pupil will then experience the safety, security and stability they need in order to take the risks necessary to become vulnerable, to learn and to extend themselves.

A **Key Teacher** needs to know and be very clear about the boundaries around her role so that she does not take on more than is necessary. I'm very aware of the intensive stress there is at the moment with so much evaluation going on within the bigger picture of education. Evaluation is known to disable and to increase stress. So it is even more important today that teachers hold their boundaries. Because the particular pupil you are working with will have a wider range of needs, you may well experience the sense of there not ever being enough for them or of not feeling good enough yourself. But rather than being blown off course, be determined to keep your focus sharp both for the welfare of this individual pupil and for the welfare of the rest of the class. I find it helpful to remember that we are alongside these pupils as fellow travellers, not as staff from the emergency services.

Within the model I am advocating throughout the **Attachment Aware School Series**, the **Key Teacher** works in parallel to the Key Adult in the classroom and around the school. It is very important that status is put aside and that you view each other as full Team members - both playing essential roles as equals. You will both really need one another. You also have the Senior Manager to refer to as the facilitator of your Team.

See yourself as the leader of learning, and the Key Adult as the expert on the individual pupil. The Key Adult will have the opportunity and privilege of finding out a lot more about this pupil than you will have the capacity for, with so many other children in mind and the sea of faces from the front of your class. The Key Adult is ideally placed to learn this pupil's story, their emotional and social age, their states, their stressors and calmers. You are ideally placed to lead on the learning front, to ensure this pupil has the right kinds of activities and interactions that will draw them in and encourage connection, rather than drive disconnection.

Whilst the Key Adult has the closest relationship with the parents and carers of the troubled pupil, **Key Teachers** will probably only have direct contact more sporadically, especially in the secondary context, for example at a Parents' Evening. Those working in primary may have much more contact depending on the way your school operates. However, your observations would be much appreciated for the weekly Home/School Prompt sheet (*see* **STL**) that the Key Adult writes up each week.

Key Adults are usually members of support staff - teaching assistants (TAs), individual needs assistants (INAs), emotional literacy support assistants (ELSAs) or mentors from the main school staff within a school. Key Adults prepare themselves to be the best **additional attachment figures** they can be for those pupils who have experienced toxic stress from pregnancy onwards, and/or have had compromised or **disrupted relationships/connections** with adults in their early years.

We now know that a history of **relational trauma and loss** needn't be a life sentence of insecure attachments, **developmental vulnerabilities**, low educational outcomes and a compromised future. Children and young people *can* learn security and can negotiate and consolidate the necessary developmental milestones. But they need us all alongside them to do so.

Education from 5 to 16 is compulsory in the UK, and so these children and young people will be with us for many weeks, terms and years. If they have been wounded '*within relationship*,' it makes sense for us to prioritise and use quality relational interventions to help them, as *relationship* is the necessary vehicle for supporting adaption and recovery.

> For many children and young people, a sense of
> connectedness with just one adult … is enough to end
> their deep sense of aloneness, isolation, not belonging,
> not being understood.   Sunderland 2015, p.19

We know now that both emotional growth and well-being are directly linked to learning. We also know that the more a child or young person experiences quality connections with mature adults, the more mature his brain becomes.

So it is the **Key Teacher's** role and professional responsibility to ensure that these pupils are seen as pupils with additional needs: that they are given appropriate learning and differentiated tasks, and that expectations based on their emotional and social age and on their executive functioning vulnerabilities (*see the* Trauma Tree *in* **WAM**) inform all interventions with pupils.

We also know from neuroscience that the richer relational experiences these pupils have, the more complex the neural pathways and connections in their brains will be, meaning that relationships bring integration. Integration brings health - physical, mental and emotional health. And richer relational experiences and more complex systems in the brain mean the pupil will be able to engage in more complex thinking, relating and being. This is the way ahead for all of us who take our pupils' well-being and development seriously. **Key Teachers** are well placed to take the lead in making this happen.

The Key Teacher in School

> Let's shift from a behavioural view of pupils to a
> relational one - focussing on trying to understand what
> their behaviour means [or communicates].
>
> Hughes & Baylin 2012, p.8 (*my parantheses*)

Up until recently, it was thought that the responsibility to support the mental health and well-being of these children and young people lay solely with their parents/carers, social workers and therapists. However, I know first-hand from many years of experience out in schools how powerful a Key Adult relationship and an assigned pupil team can be within the educational context.

Key Adults who are physically and emotionally present, attentive, attuned and responsive, provide the ground for these children and young people to thrive. And those Key Adults who also employ *playfulness*, communicate *acceptance*, engage *curiosity* and show *empathy* (Hughes, 2009, *and see* Book 1, *in this series*, **KAiS**) can actually support these children and young people into new learning, development and opportunities. The possibilities are endless!

And I also know the huge difference it makes to a pupil, to a class, to a school and to parents, if classroom teachers, subject teachers and tutors/form tutors - **Key Teachers** - are actively involved in attachment aware and trauma informed interventions. The pupils sense those who are on their side, rooting for them, believing in them, cheering them on to be all they were intended to be first time round. It is not surprising then that in your classes they respond better than maybe in the classes of one or two of your colleagues who don't understand these pupils' hidden needs - yet. You will notice the word 'yet' in a lot of my writing as our brains are experience dependent: so give a person enough of the right experiences and they update! Pupils and adults as well ...

> Teacher-student attunement is not a 'nice addition' to the learning experience but a core requirement.
>
> Cozolino 2013, p.18

To make the best use of this book, your whole school community would first ideally have had at least two full days of training in child development, attachment, neuroscience and trauma, to create a platform for effective, consistent, attachment aware practice in school. All these key principles and practices will obviously need to be re-visited on a regular basis in order to truly embed the work I'll be outlining in this book (and throughout the **Attachment Aware School Series**) into the usual ways of how we are and what we do within the school culture.

In addition, I recommend that each school allocates an interested member of support staff and Senior Management to train up as **Attachment Leads** so that they can ensure quality practice, and keep the momentum going (*see* attachmentleadnetwork.net).

A NOTE ABOUT CONSULTATION

Each of us needs to be clear as to the boundaries of our role and responsibilities. There are occasions when attachment aware interventions will not be sufficient, and a trauma informed practitioner will need to be involved for specialist assessments, advice and interventions.

Who should that individual be? I would strongly recommend a specialist therapist with complex trauma/ developmental trauma expertise. Our children and young people need appropriate professionals involved who will provide an extension to the ground work already laid down within the attachment aware practices employed by a school. This is our joint ethical responsibility. As well as detailed assessments and direct interventions, these same professionals can also provide specialist supervision to staff in school on a regular basis. Increasing staff care increases our care-giving capacity, which means that we will then be more able to facilitate the permanency that our pupils need. By facilitating and honouring the vehicle of relationship, we will be 'respecting biology' (Perry, 2014).

It will be the **Key Teacher's** responsibility to work on their own understanding of self so that they can be the best they can for these pupils: to learn all they can about this area of additional need: and to stay connected with the others in Team Pupil. I feel it's also important to say here that as adults working in this field, we do have an ethical responsibility to take care of our own personal histories, so that our own unresolved traumas and losses don't get re-enacted in the classroom with vulnerable pupils. If that means journalling, opening up to others or even therapy, so be it. In order to be the most effective teachers we can be with these pupils, we need to stay regulated and well.

Do consider attending Team Pupil support groups if they run in your area, similar to those I've set up in Brighton perhaps. They will help you remember you are not alone and that those in neighbouring schools face the same challenges and experience the same rewarding moments as you will. Relationship enables us all to thrive.

The Key Teacher in School

Part One

Becoming an attachment aware Key Teacher

The aim of this book

This book is focused on the **Key Teachers** involved with pupils identified as needing additional support, due to **the relational stress, trauma** and losses they have experienced in their short lives to date. These pupils need rich relational interventions from adults in school in order to adapt and recover: then they will be able to move towards learned security, and be better able to settle to learn.

These children and young people have experienced ruptures in their relationships, some have even been wounded within relationship. They have developed fixed ways of thinking and feeling about themselves, grown-ups and the contexts they find themselves in, based on these ruptures and hurt. Such ways of thinking and feeling are distortions of the current reality they experience in school, and left alone, they are unlikely to change these perspectives. Within Team Pupil, **Key Teachers** can now come alongside these pupils. Our job is to ensure they are no longer alone; it is to gently challenge their perceptions of themselves and others (especially grown-ups) through our strong presence and sensitive attunement in the classroom.

What does a Key Teacher do in the attachment aware context - and why?

Key Teachers are ideally placed to lead, create, inspire, notice, journey, hope for and be alongside these troubled pupils. Let's examine this value system or map together, so that you can begin this important role believing in everything you can offer, simply by being you.

LEAD As a **Key Teacher** you are in a privileged position: in effect, you are a leader, leading the way into growth, into development, into relationships, into work, into all kinds of pathways in life.

CREATE You are ideally placed to open up and facilitate all kinds of opportunities for extending these pupils. Your creativity will be key.

INSPIRE You will be watched *all* the time. Your passion and care will not go unnoticed. These pupils will experience you as a mirror of who they are now, and a witness to all they could become.

NOTICE As a **Key Teacher** at the front of a class
or leading your subject you observe so much.
Over time, you will notice the optimal conditions
needed to engage these particular pupils'
curiosity and their focus.

JOURNEY You will probably spend at least an
academic year with this pupil, possibly longer. In
the life of a child, this is an eternity. Don't ever
under-play or under-estimate the time you will
have together. Make the most of the journey.
Your pupil needs to know they are not alone, and
they won't be, since you will be alongside them
for this critical part of their lives.

HOPE   As a **Key Teacher** with all your existing and
growing knowledge, you will have the confidence
to believe in the resourcefulness of the human
brain. Your pupil will catch a sense of this, even if
it is 'simply' communicated implicitly. Pupils who
have experienced relational trauma and loss are
anything but stupid. They know who believes in
their capacity to thrive, and who doesn't.

If we treat people as they are, we make them worse.
If we treat people as they ought to be, we help them
become what they are capable of becoming.
    variously attributed both to Goethe and Viktor Frankl

The Key Teacher in School

The quote above was at the beginning of my education dissertation in my final year many, many years ago when I was completing my Bachelor of Education. I was determined to work with this perspective throughout my teaching career from my final teaching practice in Toxteth onwards! And I'm pleased to say I think I have (so far!) and many, many pupils along the way have experienced me getting alongside them, rooting for them and holding onto hope for them. I dream that every teacher can realise the power of relationship, and especially hope. Bearing this in mind, many of us in education who have similar beliefs have witnessed pupils soften up or 'defrost' over time, becoming increasingly vulnerable and teachable.

Even in deserts, the most barren of places on this planet, there is life. In the concrete jungles we have built in the inner city, shoots of grass still push their way through the pavement cracks (Regan 2015). It is the same for our pupils who have experienced relational trauma and loss. They have erected defences which are very strong. Sometimes we all find ourselves wondering whether this time we'll ever get through to them, as they seem so resistant. *But there is always hope,* and I hope this book and the others in the **Attachment Aware School Series** will help you hold onto yours.

Core aims of teachers in Team Pupil

The Key Teacher's aims are to

1   build relationship with the pupil who is the focus of Team Pupil

2   facilitate the most conducive environment for learning for this pupil in your class or subject area

3   co-ordinate the focus of the Individual Development Plan with the Key Adult

4   engage the pupil's further interest in one or two key curricular areas (already identified as strengths)

5   notice and draw attention to their development tentatively, being wary not to overwhelm with praise (see **IIH, WAM** and **STL**)

6   be mindful of others in your class/classes that may not have been identified formally as presenting with attachment difficulties, but who would still benefit from an attachment aware and trauma informed approach.

The Key Teacher in School

> **7** be generous to the rest of Team Pupil in your opinions, views and actions so that there is harmony between each member of the team and everyone can think clearly and well.

Ideal qualities of an attachment aware Key Teacher

Patient ☆ Kind ☆ Wise

Smiling, eyes saying "yes"

Boundaried ☆ Sense of humor ☆ Creative

Warm body language

Flexible ☆ Gently challenging ☆ Regulated

High but achievable expectations

Playful ☆ Active listener ☆ Inspirational

Not easily threatened

Open ☆ Team player ☆ Nurturing

Comfortable in their own skin

Healthy self esteem ☆ Robust ☆ Persevering

Good questions about attachment aware Key Teachers

↳ *Should teachers lower their expectations when a pupil has problems then?*

No, certainly not! Let's be consistent, but not rigid. These pupils need our flexibility and they need creative approaches. Remember they have spikey profiles, so there'll be times when challenge needs to be reduced and nurture increased. We need to provide a careful interplay between nurture and gentle challenge. The more attuned you are to the pupil, the better this attachment dance between you will go.

↳ *What about teacher performance and Ofsted?*

When working with these pupils it is very important that you document their starting point - their history of **relational trauma** and loss, their initial difficulties/vulnerabilities in class, the interventions you're using and what has changed or is changing. We cannot afford to drift with these pupils. We need to be as focused as possible, clear about why we are doing what we are doing and why we are not using other interventions. Confidence and clarity go a long way. Be one of the brave ones out there within education who stand firm. Explain that these pupils need our time as they are on a recovery journey, and that the work cannot be fast-tracked. If you are evaluated, use this as an opportunity to educate others.

The Key Teacher in School

↳ *What about the others in the class?*

Ensure you work especially hard at celebrating difference and diversity in your class/es. The more pupils understand how we are all different and unique the more they will tolerate. You can tell which schools have established ground in this area, as the pupils there don't bat an eyelid even if they observe the stressed presentation of a pupil such as Jack: they know Jack struggles with stress, as he experienced too much when he was very young.

Do use any opportunities you can to educate the whole class in how our nervous systems work (*see* p.51). The more we all learn about our alarm systems and how they work the better. More knowledge in this area can lead to better understanding and patience.

↳ *Who should be disciplining the pupil?*

Discipline should only happen through Team Pupil, but ensure you're all in agreement as to the best approach. Remember that toxic shame is the foundation you are having to work with (*see* **Glossary**), so our pupils won't need any more shame and definitely no humiliation of any kind. We need to work hard at being the best stress and shame regulators we can be. Remember to also focus on the connection between you and the pupil before any kind of correction. It may also be necessary to attend to the regulation of the pupil even before that too, as they need to be in the right state to hear what you are saying. Discipline is really teaching, so think about how best you might teach this pupil what they need to know in order to function well within the class and school community. A great book that I would strongly recommend is *No Drama Discipline* (Siegel 2015). Every school needs this book. When you do discipline, reduce your words and use short phrases. Don't be tempted to threaten. Just commentate on what's happening, and, most importantly, provide an exit strategy and ensure you both use it together! For example - "*We could … or we could …*"

↳ *What should I say when the child or young person (the focus of Team Pupil) asks about my work with other pupils, or whether I like other pupils?*

Be boundaried and ensure that you tell your pupil that when you're with him, you talk with him about him and him alone: it's his time. Don't be tempted to talk about any other children or young people you either parent or teach, as this will only fuel your pupil's anxiety, though they don't realise that that is what is driving their questions.

10 things others in Team Pupil say about

When you have an understanding **teacher** on board the work is so much easier. (KA)

He was so chuffed to have his favourite **teacher** on his team. He can't quite get that we are all rooting for him but he is starting to smile a lot more! (KA)

This **teacher** has taken the time to really listen and understand my child's story. I know we are going to have a good year. (Carer)

Because consistency is key, knowing the **teacher** is on board and I don't have to keep explaining myself means that the child can feel secure, knowing we are working as part of a team. (KA)

Billy knows that this **teacher** really believes in him. He loves art and she has focused in on this, so much so that he is now talking about enjoying school when previously he didn't want to come. (KA)

attachment aware Key Teachers

She can be very challenging but this teacher has stuck in there with her and we can all see the positive impact this has had in her behavior and learning. (SM)

Everyone knows that when certain pupils have particular teachers, they are so much more settled and able to learn. (SM)

When you have an empathic teacher on board who also excels in their subject area you know you have the chance to make a difference in a young person's life. (SM)

I'm going to get a job now as I know the teacher is not fazed by Lucy and knows what she needs in order to be regulated in the classroom. (Parent)

She has a good teacher, one who is nurturing but also firm. She knows where she is with this teacher. (SM)

The Key Teacher in School

Part Two

The attachment aware Key Teacher

Teachers need to be protected to teach. Classes are large nowadays, and there is so much to do. However, you will also be playing a significant role for this key child or young person within Team Pupil. You will be the hope bearer! You will be the one who imagines everything that could happen if these pupils are provided with an attuned relationship and attended to by their Key Adults. And you will be in the best possible place to strengthen the pupil's strengths and abilities, their resilience factors.

What a role you have! You will be on the frontline to witness what a difference following the 3 R's can make - Regulate, Relate and Reason. By this I mean that I see it as our responsibility to first *regulate* (in other words to soothe, calm and stabilise the pupil); then *relate* through connection, and then finally to find a way to discuss *reason* with them (Perry

2014). By doing this, in this order, we are respecting the biology of the troubled pupil in front of us, and supporting their development.

Whether others understand or not, our first responsibility is to the pupil. This will mean that we may often need to delay our use of discipline until we have attended to the first two R's - those of Regulation and Relationship - so there may be a time lapse between them. We can only effectively use the third R linked to discipline - Reason - when - (and only when) the pupil is in the right state to make sense of the discipline, and to make good use of it for future times. Please remember that the Key Adult will lead on this sequence, but as a **Key Teacher,** you do need to have an awareness of it to understand what he or she is doing.

You are also ideally placed to be one of the first to experience first-hand how the **exploratory system** of a pupil (used for learning) who has experienced **relational trauma** and loss can come online if their **attachment system** (needed for security and relationship) is well attended to. You will see evidence over time of pupils becoming more settled in themselves, more fully engaged with the curriculum and actually beginning to realise their potential in whatever their 'element' is (*see* p.34).

Being part of Team Pupil is bound to affect your practice with all pupils for many years to come. And if you can work with Jade or Kevin, you can work with anyone! Your confidence will increase, and the troubled pupils will pick up on your strong presence in the classroom. They will then feel psychologically 'held' within a system that is usually riddled with impermanency, stress and challenge. Feeling psychologically held means being able to have a felt sense of safety. This can only lead to better outcomes in the classroom in terms of behaviour and learning.

Key functions of Key Teachers

I   LIAISE WITH THE OTHERS IN TEAM PUPIL, ESPECIALLY THE KEY ADULT

Do allow the Key Adult to lead on behalf of the pupil's everyday needs, stressors and calmers. You need to focus on the overall plan decided within Team Pupil for how to settle these pupils to learn. However, do join in with complementing everything they are doing to reinforce their work. Your Key Pupil needs to know that you are all equal members of the same team. Pass on to the Key Adult any stressors or calmers you have observed over the week and any possible stressors for next week, so that the Key Adult can complete the Home/School Partnership form on Fridays (*and see* Home/School sheet template *in* **STL**).

If you work in the primary phase, ensure you set up a time to introduce yourself to the parent/carer outside of Parents' Evenings or other set events where there may be a lot of people around. This particular parent/carer needs to feel confident that you are rooting for their child or young person, doing all you can to unlock their learning potential that has usually been so compromised by relational stress, trauma and loss.

If you work in the secondary phase, initiate contact by email to introduce yourself as part of Team Pupil. These parent/ carers need to have some kind of contact to know that you are working hard in class to help these pupils be all they were intended to be, first time round.

Make sure you clarify in both phases that the Key Adult will be the main point of contact, but that any concerns - and celebrations - will be passed on to everyone in Team Pupil. This ensures consistency and integrated support, as schools are now such large learning communities and we need to create smaller worlds for these particular pupils (*see* **SMiS**).

Check in with the Team Pupil Senior Manager on a consistent basis to let them know your perspective on this pupil's development, their progress, how they are interacting with you, with the Key Adult and with their peers. Let the Senior Manager know of anything you can see that is getting stronger, especially any emerging patterns you've observed.

2   BUILD RELATIONSHIP

Your Key Pupil needs to experience you as warm and open in both your body language and in what you communicate. Connection is key to settling these pupils into school and into their learning, so invest time wherever and whenever you can. The quality moments here and there really are significant. The smile, the pat on the shoulder, your warm smiley eyes, the encouraging *"Yes"*:   you noticing what others might not ...

These pupils are going to need huge amounts of relentless care and a belief that they will make it through, no matter what.   We can't promise to take away any difficulties, hurdles, vulnerabilities or stress. However, we can promise companionship.   They need to know they're not alone on their marathon journeys through education.   They need supporters on the sidelines, walking alongside, encouraging them to keep going.   They need to know that together we can learn to 'surf the waves' (Johnstone 2012) and that you'll pass on tools and strategies for this.   Our troubled pupils are hypervigilant and will be watching, so let's give them lots to ponder!   Your very being could significantly challenge their perceptions of grown-ups. Please remember they don't trust adults.   They don't realise that you're on their side and wouldn't necessarily recognise that you are rooting for them!

3   FACILITATE THE MOST CONDUCIVE ENVIRONMENT FOR LEARNING

Learn the child.   Think about your classroom.   What could you do to facilitate a stress-free environment?   In fact, an environment that feels really comfortable?   Do you need to increase sensory comfort in any way?   I would strongly recommend that you read *School as a Secure Base* (Street 2014) to raise your awareness of the many possibilities we can attend to.   Think of lighting, air flow, seating arrangements, stress relievers, background sounds and sights ... start experimenting, and notice what seems to support this particular pupil to focus (*and see* p.81).

4   USE THE INDIVIDUAL DEVELOPMENT PLAN (IDP) AS A WORKING DOCUMENT

It's important that each of the pupils who have been identified as needing Team Pupil has an individual development plan.   It can be brief (*please see* **WAM**) or a more detailed one such as Seguridad from TouchBase™ (*see* **Useful Contacts**), when a trauma therapist becomes involved.   The Senior Manager or **Attachment Lead** will have led on the creation of the brief IDP (*see* **STL** *for template*) but you'll need to ensure this is now used as a working document for all teaching and learning.

If there is a more detailed plan, you will play an important role in ensuring that the team stay focused, and that no-one loses sight of your joint objectives and the inspiration behind supporting your Key Pupil together. And at all times, their pace of development needs to be honoured. Please note that just because academic years are divided into terms does not mean that the pupil's developmental pace will necessarily fit this. In fact, when you are deciding to gently challenge them further in terms of their development in a particular area, please don't do this at the beginning of a half-term or full term. Stagger all shifts in expectations and contexts, as beginnings and endings all have their own challenges and can activate their nervous systems. For a pupil who already has an overwhelmed and fragile nervous system, timings are very significant!

5 CONSIDER THE CHALLENGES AND OPPORTUNITIES OF THE CURRICULUM

Let's be aware of possible curriculum triggers. Walk a mile in this pupil's shoes and consider the possible emotional impact of work on families, celebrations, losses, terror/ trauma/disasters/wars and so on, in relation to this pupil's starting point, by checking out this pupil's Factfile (*see* **WAM**, *and* Part 3, *below*, p.88).

But it is also all too easy for us to fall into the habit of only focussing on the Key Pupil's **developmental vulnerabilities**. Instead, let's notice where they feel most comfortable, where they excel, what switches them on, what engages their curiosity, and then, alongside them, build further momentum to engage with these interests and strengths more regularly during the school day and week.

I've found Ken Robinson's book *The Element* really helpful here (2010). It really supports us to follow pupil's gifts, talents and strengths which can often go unnoticed in our fast paced, full-on national curriculum. The other book I recommend is *The Invisible Classroom*, Olson (2014). He suggests helpful ways to identify what each pupil's strengths are.

Whatever it is - whatever your Key Pupil's passion - ensure that he or she has opportunity to engage with it at least once daily. Don't wait until the art lesson on Thursday if your Key Pupil excels in art. Instead, enable him or her to do something creative every day.

Inspire these pupils. Model how to work with or engage with an area of interest. Give them additional support in their area of strength if at all possible, to invest into their resilience. For example, invite the pupil to come in before form starts or at lunchtime to show them something related to what they are interested in or to tell them about that art exhibition that would engage their interest further.

An enhanced curriculum will set these pupils up to succeed, and will support the development of a robust sense of self. Join in and celebrate what makes them smile and begin to develop good feelings about themselves.

6 NOTICE DEVELOPMENT

It will be very important that you keep an overview of the pupil's starting point in terms of their background, their presenting behaviours, the strategies being employed and the changes you are noticing. I call this the *Four Slide case presentation*. Notice the growth of anything that is healthy and appropriate, for example anything that might indicate that your Key Pupil might be starting to trust the grown-ups in school. Feed this back to Team Pupil, but also to your Key Pupil from time to time. But be wary to only give him or her small doses of good things, including praise. Pupils with backgrounds of **relational trauma** and loss can so easily move into overwhelm if they receive too much evaluation - positive or negative. You may well find that using phrases such as 'practising'and 'getting stronger at' go down much better, as such language is not shame-based.

7 MODEL AND ADVOCATE FOR ATTACHMENT AWARE AND TRAUMA INFORMED PRACTICES

Other colleagues will be interested in what you are doing and are bound to ask you questions. Engage their curiosity by advocating for these approaches and practices with all pupils who are hurting. Optimise opportunities to share examples of good practice especially when you have observed shifts. Explain that behaviour is a megaphone for communication, and that we need to translate what these pupils might say if they could express themselves in a more healthy and appropriate way. Encourage others to have a go at approaching difficulties in the classroom in a different way. It requires courage, as these approaches do take you out of the familiar into territories unfamiliar and unknown: but encourage others to dip their toe in and try as well! Use the chart on p.44 to help them to understand some of the key differences between different approaches:

Responsibilities of Key Teachers

▷ Integrate *regulate, relate and reason* principles and practices into all planning of lesson delivery

▷ *Differentiate* for social and emotional tasks and expectations as well as for learning. Do not be fazed by the mismatch emotionally and socially in relation to the pupil's chronological age

▷ Recognise the nature of the 'Big Ask' that we make of these pupils (see p.52)

▷ View behaviour as communication: have a go at translating for these pupils in the best way you can

▷ Be determined that when these pupils are on your watch that you will act as a stress and shame regulator so that they do not become overwhelmed

▷ Remember that what comes your way is not intended for you, but for someone else in another time and another space. It may well 'feel' personal, but it really isn't

▷ Remember key aspects about the pupil to bring up from time to time so that the pupil feels 'known'

▷ Use open-ended reflective type questions, and give yourself and your pupil space and time to respond

▷ Remember that this pupil is always watching, so give them the positive evidence they need to help them update how they experience adults

▷ Expect the Key Adult to be the expert on the pupil, without feeling threatened by the close relationship they develop together

▷ Treat each member of Team Pupil as equals, and support each other, recognising that we are 'all in this together'

▷ Inspire the pupil. Model how to engage with areas of strength or interest

▷ Know when to move up the 'Pyramid' of attachment aware support, and ask for more advanced input, for example an assessment and plan from a trauma therapist, when the need for it becomes apparent (*see overleaf*)

▷ Focus on your Key Pupil's hidden needs rather than the ones he or she seems to be presenting, as pupils who have experienced relational trauma and loss often become very skilled at hiding. For example, though the pupil in your class makes out they don't need your help, find as many ways as you can to help him!

The Key Teacher in School

Attachment aware and trauma informed support for those who are hurting in schools

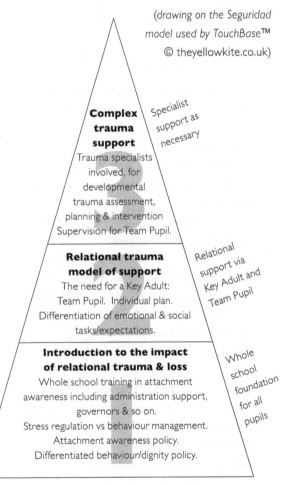

(drawing on the Seguridad model used by TouchBase™ © theyellowkite.co.uk)

Complex trauma support
Trauma specialists involved, for developmental trauma assessment, planning & intervention Supervision for Team Pupil.

Specialist support as necessary

Relational trauma model of support
The need for a Key Adult: Team Pupil. Individual plan. Differentiation of emotional & social tasks/expectations.

Relational support via Key Adult and Team Pupil

Introduction to the impact of relational trauma & loss
Whole school training in attachment awareness including administration support, governors & so on.
Stress regulation vs behaviour management.
Attachment awareness policy.
Differentiated behaviour/dignity policy.

Whole school foundation for all pupils

▷ Upskill yourself. Keep reading around this specialism. Look out for good clips on YouTube.
▷ Check in with your **Attachment Leads** in school on a regular basis to ensure you are on the right track, as when we are tired and stressed we may regress to our default position which may be a more behaviourist approach; this would not be helpful (*see p.44 and check out* attachmentleads.net).

The Key Teacher in School

If other parents question what is going on with a particular pupil

Attachment aware and trauma informed practices in schools are still relatively new ideas and concepts in the UK, so you may well be questioned from time to time. A helpful strategy is to set up a Parent Drop-in, whereby parents can have the opportunity to catch up on the latest research in this area. Invite your **Attachment Leads** (if you have them) to lead on this, or a Senior Manager if not. Together facilitate a dialogue about your school ethos, celebrating difference and diversity. Use this time as an opportunity for health promotion. The key areas to cover are:

- The brain and how the nervous system works, including our alarm systems
- How relational stress/trauma and loss can interrupt healthy development
- How connection is at the heart of all adaption and recovery, and how recovery happens
- How different tools and strategies are needed for supporting those affected by relational trauma and loss

Do consider inviting parents and carers to training events your school puts on in relation to this additional need and even consider putting on special events just for them. Do connect in with the Virtual School in your area as well, as they may well have additional literature and services you can signpost parents to.

The Circle of Security website is a great resource for parents (*see* **Glossary** *and* **Useful Contacts**), especially the connection and shark music animations that can be seen on YouTube.

Attachment aware practices vs behaviour management

Pupils who have experienced relational trauma and loss are not ready yet for behaviourist approaches and practices. These pupils have **developmental vulnerabilities** due to ruptures in relationships and having experienced **toxic stress**. Instead, go for the principles and practices outlined in this book and across the **Attachment Aware School Series**. Your pupil is letting you know he or she has a fragile sense of self, so our aim is to support him or her to build a robust sense of self.

Our pupils are letting us know that they have poor internal controls at the moment, so our aim is to support them to experience and then practise strengthening their internal controls - the brake on their inner alarm system. We all learn this in the context of relational experience. You can't be merely taught it, and that's why Team Pupil is essential! If a pupil has previously been wounded in relationship, then healthy relationship with a mature and empathic adult will be the vehicle towards adaption and recovery, not another behaviour chart with targets and rewards attached. Charts of this kind are far too simplistic and can actually exacerbate a problematic situation. Deep down these pupils know they need to be seen, known and understood so that they can belong and survive. We were all born for connection. When we are connected, we are healthy and well. When we are connected, we 'operate' optimally and are then freed to use our brain's **exploratory system** - the system necessary for learning.

So let's do all we can to facilitate and strengthen connection rather than continuing to engage in activities that drive disconnection - taking things away, time out, seclusion, isolation. These pupils already have a deep sense of scarcity. Why would we want to collude with that? Let's surprise them with our generosity, warmth and understanding. Let's provide relational proximity rather than relational withdrawal all the time, but especially at times of increased stress. Remember we are now stress regulators not behaviour managers, as I've mentioned at different points throughout this book. Please look at the chart on pp.44-5 to really be clear about the difference between the attachment aware and trauma informed approach, and a behaviourist one.

Some helpful starter phrases for tricky dynamics

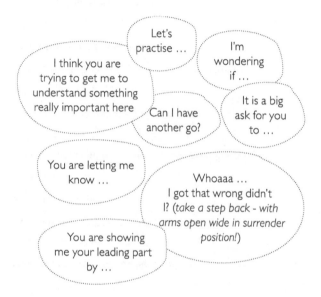

I think you are trying to get me to understand something really important here

Let's practise ...

I'm wondering if ...

It is a big ask for you to ...

Can I have another go?

You are letting me know ...

Whoaaa ... I got that wrong didn't I? *(take a step back - with arms open wide in surrender position!)*

You are showing me your leading part by ...

To extend these further, do read *Conversations That Matter* by Dr Margot Sunderland (2015).

The Key Teacher in School

ATTACHMENT AWARE AND
TRAUMA INFORMED APPROACH IN SCHOOL

Facilitating relative dependency

Creating emotional safety through sensitive attuned care

Becoming stress managers

The adult being responsible for holding boundaries

Flexibility of approach

Focussing on strengthening a pupil's internal controls

Encouraging relational proximity - time in for the pupil

Being responsive

Being preventative

Expectations and tasks based on emotional
and social age of pupil

Adapting the environment to the pupil

All transitions to be identified and prepared for

Accountability for the processes used by education staff

Using the pupil's history so far as a framework
in which to interpret behaviour

Strengthening a pupil's sense of self

Using relational influence to create motivation

Attending to the attachment needs of the pupil

VS BEHAVIOURAL APPROACH

vs **encouraging further pseudo independence**

vs the use of more authority, power, control

vs **managing behaviour**

vs more consequences for the pupil

vs **rigidity of approach**

vs imposing external controls that the pupil might not be developmentally ready for yet

vs **relational withdrawal or distance - time out for the pupil**

vs being reactive

vs **being crisis driven**

vs expectations and tasks being matched to the pupil's chronological age

vs **expecting the pupil to adapt to the existing environment**

vs only identifying the major transitions that a pupil might face

vs **only accountability for performance/outcome of pupils**

vs blank canvass approach

vs **assuming the pupil is robust enough to manage everyday opportunities and stressors**

vs the use of rewards and sanctions to create motovation

vs **assuming all attachment needs have been met**

Developed from Forbes 2012, p.178 for the UK education system

The Key Teacher in School

Part Three

Moving forwards

So you've been asked to be part of Team Pupil for a vulnerable child or young person. How are you feeling, now you have more of a sense of what's involved? You may be a little daunted by the prospect, especially in view of your already demanding responsibilities and the ever-growing expectations in the classroom right now.

So at this point, let's de-mystify the role a little. It's important to flag up that it isn't about adding to your pressure and stress, but about re-jigging the relational dynamics that are probably around already to ensure that you, your allocated Key Pupil and the rest of your class/es are enabled to make the most of every day at school. Time is precious. None of us want our time to be wasted.

The Key Teacher in School

Basically this particular pupil is going to need a champion. You've been identified as someone who could play quite a significant role in supporting him or her to realise that they are safe to venture out beyond what is known and familiar into new unchartered territories: in other words, to move on into more advanced levels of learning. As I have described, the pupil may be quite reluctant to truly open herself to new learning, to engage her **exploratory system**, because of all the stress she has already experienced. Sadly, most of the stress has been relational. But in order to optimise our exploratory systems, we all need to experience a good dose of felt safety, security and stability in our relationships. So that's what she needs now.

You won't be alone. You'll be able to work with the other members of Team Pupil to give your pupil the opportunity to experience rich, relational interventions, which can 'tame' them into wanting exploration. If and when we see their curiosity being awakened, we'll know that their **exploratory system** is beginning to come online.

Your passion for your subject or subject/s will play a big part in the support work, and your relationship with your Key Pupil will as well. This pupil needs you to dream big dreams on her behalf and to imagine all she could become. She will pick up very quickly whether you are on her side or not, and whether you believe in her or not.

Let's think about fear …

I realise that the word 'fear' is not probably going to be one that you might consider when bringing a pupil who has experienced **relational trauma** and loss to mind. You're probably more likely to pick a word from this list:

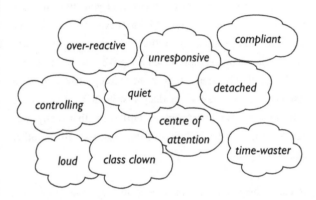

So you may be surprised to hear that in fact, research clearly shows us that fear fuels most of the behaviors that we see. Fear can masquerade in all kinds of ways, including the things I've described above. Sadly, the smokescreen that accompanies fear often doesn't get identified as such in our schools, and so many pupils don't receive the kind of support that they desperately need in order to function. But we must recognise that these pupils have experienced such a lot of powerlessness and fear during their short lives to date. If you check out their Factfiles, perhaps you'll get more of a sense of why this might be the case. There'll you'll find events and experiences such as neglect, emotional, physical, sexual abuse, parental addiction or medical difficulties, moving from birth parents, losing a parent, escaping from war, witnessing atrocities … I could go on.

Even the most compliant child can fool you into thinking the trauma has disappeared and that they are OK and don't need any help, especially if they're now living in a safe environment, for example in an adoptive family. But let's think again! Of course they want to keep grown-ups at a distance. They have been deeply wounded. Many have determined never to let anyone hurt them that badly ever again. You will be included in this, just like all the other adults in school.

Because they have so much fear inside, these pupils are going to need big doses of sensitively attuned care. Many teachers have been misinformed and taught that poorly behaved children need increasingly assertive discipline and better behavior management. Whilst that might be true with pupils who have experienced 'good enough' care, this type of approach can actually exacerbate difficulties in pupils who have experienced an overdose of relational stress and are traumatised in some way. Many have learned how to keep grown-ups at some distance to defend their weakness, vulnerability and powerlessness. Of course they feel the need to hide. This is the best survival strategy to use when you are filled with fear.

So in our work I am going to recommend that you imagine the fear. It will help you to have some kind of sensory expression of your pupil's fear, because it can't be seen and is often so well hidden. So give it a colour. Give it a shape. Give it a sound. Give it a smell. When you're working with your particular pupil, do all you can to remember their fear. It will really support your work.

Let's understand about alarm

In order to be an effective support as part of Team Pupil, you, your pupil and the other pupils around will need to understand about how the alarm system in each one of us works. We all need to be familiar with how parts of the brain known as the amygdala and the hippocampus in particular work. This is going to need to be included in the curriculum, in an age-appropriate way. A great book to support understanding is *Help! I've got an alarm going off in my head* by Louisa Aspden (2015). You'll find some theory and lots of practical ideas for how to put the brakes on when your alarm is activated.

The pupils we are concerned about have internal and external triggers going off that readily switch on an already over-active alarm system, because of all the previous alarm they have lived through. So they are often going to feel led by their bodies (rather than their minds) into all kinds of defensive strategies. It's not nice to feel 'out of control. It is actually frightening for any of us. Being out of control also leaves you with high levels of shame. These pupils already have toxic levels of shame, so this can make everything so much worse. As you can imagine this all perpetuates a vicious spiral, and a misattuned response from an adult to the beginnings of behavioural disruption can simply make that cycle speed up and the situation escalate.

However, the cycle can be broken if a kind and wise teacher gets alongside, and teaches the pupil about what is going on and what can help. We all know that if we are educated we feel more empowered. The same goes for our pupils. We can actually help them apply the brakes. Together we can give them the resources to know what to do.

The Marathon ... The Big Ask

I think we all need to be mindful that coming to school is something like a marathon for these pupils. They can't just get going. There are so many Big Asks in school. Opposite I've listed just some of these; I'm sure you could add to this list!

In Brighton we have a marathon every year. Most of those who enter the race do well and have prepared long and hard for this day. I think we can take a lot from this preparation to help us know what our pupils are going to need in school.

They are going to need a 'coach' who believes in them and roots for them. They are going to need training that is personal, paced and achievable. They are going to need practice that extends over time so that they can become stronger and function better. They are going to need nurture and encouragement to keep going by us noticing what they can now do (for example noticing out loud, the Jar of Strength and the Book of Success, *see* **IIH, WAM**). They will also need us cheering them on at the finishing line, acknowledging how far they have come.

The Big Ask in school

Being self- and other-aware in order to make wise choices **FEELING SAFE**

B e i n g
f r e e
f r o m
t o x i c
s h a m e   **Having a feeling of belonging**

TRUSTING GROWN-UPS

Relinquishing some control to grown-ups   *Being freed up enough*

Being free from anxiety   *to engage in*

FEELING SPECIAL AND SIGNIFICANT   *curiosity and exploration*

Taking the risks required in learning

Following the lead of grown-ups

Negotiating key developmental stages such as adolescence   *Managing multiple transitions*

Managing sensory overload

The Key Teacher in School

What our pupils need

▷   A Key Adult who forms a meaningful and genuine relationship with them on a 1:1 basis

▷   Relationally rich context in class and throughout school: Team Pupil

▷   Sensory interventions on a regular basis

▷   Adults who are able to provide state dependent interventions

▷   Adults who encourage and facilitate playfulness whatever the pupil's age

▷   Relentless care

▷   Nurture and gentle challenge

What our pupils DON'T need

✘   Adults increasing their power, authority and control

✘   Relational control

✘   Stress

✘   Shaming

✘   'One size fits all' approaches

✘   Rigidity

✘   External controls such as stickers, charts, points

Helpful interventions maximise opportunities for relationships and regulation.

Team work

It is so important that we share these pointers with our colleagues and with parents/carers so that everyone can understand what is most helpful for our pupils. Remember our aim is to support them to function at both home and school. Some of the above suggestions would be helpful for all the pupils in our classes! However they are especially a lifeline for troubled pupils who have been wounded within relationships.

10 things children and young people say about attachment aware Key Teachers

I knew she believed in me

She just seemed to get it

She was the only one who understood me

Lighten up a bit. I realise some of what you say needs to be serious, but let us know that learning can be fun too

Have a calm tone to you

They seemed to be like friends somehow

She used to check in on me, you know, just to see if I was doing OK

She had her eye on me but you know I liked it. I felt like she cared

At my old school no-one would even notice if I was in the class or not, now I feel like I'm meant to be there

She listened

A PROTECTING YOUR ROLE

There are three aspects to this: preserving your professional role as a teacher per se: being clear about your work with your Key Pupil, and about how you will look after yourself. At this time, more than ever, it is so important that you protect your role - the relational aspect of being a teacher. When you first started out I expect you were imagining that connecting to your pupils would be a significant contributor to their learning in your classroom. That was my plan when I started teaching. However, over time, with all the demands on us as teachers, relationship can be compromised. I found that it was hard to get to know the children in my class well as there was always something else demanding my attention, for example the latest literacy scheme. A conscious choice is therefore needed to ensure quality time with pupils.

I've mentioned the huge amount of evaluation within the teaching profession, undoubtedly causing higher levels of anxiety than is helpful. Remember the greater our anxiety, the more we start functioning from the lower parts of our brain. We're more likely to come out with more primitive reactions and make more egocentric choices. Not a helpful place to work from! We need to protect our capacity for reflective functioning, that is, our ability to think about what we're feeling, what is happening and what is needed. So whatever we can do to counter the build-up of our own anxiety and the anxiety in our classrooms and corridors will be helpful. The more aware we are of what is going on systemically within our school systems the better, as this will mean we have more chance to make healthy choices.

When we're fearful, all human beings have the capacity to switch off and become more robotic in our functioning. Yet all through the **Attachment Aware School Series** I describe how these pupils need rich relational interventions in order to have the opportunity to recover from significant **relational traumas** and losses. So the big question is how you and I, and all the teachers working in attachment aware schools, can protect ourselves and support each other, so that we are in the best place to provide what is needed for our most troubled pupils.

We need to bring *our whole selves* into this work. The more integrated we can be the better, in terms of our interests, strengths and skills. Let's share with our pupils our true selves, ourselves, in our chosen professional element of teaching. Don't let's allow pressure to drive us to be people we're not and don't want to become. Let's be true to ourselves. These pupils need those who will journey alongside them as fellow human beings, as fellow travellers.

How can we do this?

QUALITY MOMENTS catch a moment with a pupil and be mindfully present as you interact with him or her. Block all other distractions and focus on the pupil, actively listening.

The Key Teacher in School

CELEBRATE LIFE whenever you can, look for aspects
of the pupil's life to celebrate. The first time they
did a backward flip on their skateboard, their
winning goal ... Comment on it. Let them know
you are interested.

MATCHING if you notice something that you do,
think or see in a similar way to this pupil let them
know. For example: "*I like purple too!*"

SHARE SOMETHING be a little vulnerable and let the
pupil know something you have struggled with
that you can now do better.

REMEMBER be the pupil's memory bank. Use "*Do
you remember when ...?*" to support the pupil to
hold onto the 'good stuff'.

Some ideas to help strengthen your relationship with the pupil

▷ Notice and acknowledge your Key Pupil by name:
   affirm and validate him/her
▷ Learn the pupil - stressors, calmers, interests,
   states, what matters to him/her
▷ Sit alongside, not opposite. Have a strong but
   gentle presence. helping the pupil feel safe and held
▷ Be very conscious to communicate an open body

language. Don't cross your arms or legs

▷ Keep a calm tone about you. Stay grounded and breathe. Be warm and empathic

▷ Initiate contact rather than waiting for the pupil to approach you

▷ Actively listen using your whole body, not just your ears!

▷ Smile and laugh whenever you can - be playful whenever possible

▷ Facilitate opportunities to strengthen the pupil's safety, security and stability

▷ Regulate, relate and then reason - in this order

▷ Learn how to use Nurture group and Theraplay® principles and practices (see **Useful Contacts**)

▷ Know the pupil's developmental stage - think toddler!

▷ Be physically and emotionally present, attentive, attuned and responsive to the pupil

▷ Hold your boundaries; be consistent, but not rigid. Don't ever demand eye contact

▷ Use visual and kinaesthetic approaches in learning as much as possible

▷ Watch the pupil's state and use appropriate interventions at each level

▷ Do not use power, authority and control. Instead, learn how to use PACE at all times (see p.92 *and* **STL**)

▷ Use different creative media as much as you can - art, music, dance, storytelling, film

The Key Teacher in School

▷ See distractions as attempts to self-soothe
   because the pupil is feeling uncomfortable
▷ Leave out Calm Box bits and pieces especially
   when needing to talk about the serious stuff
▷ Translate as much as possible ... "*You are letting
   me know: I'm wondering*" (see **IIH**)
▷ Support these pupils to practice dependency
   first: Use follow/lead/follow/lead when you sense
   the pupil doesn't trust you and there is a battle
   for control (see **STL**)
▷ Make the most of any opportunities for nurture
   or empathic responses even for the invisible hurts
▷ Say "*Sorry*" whenever possible, and "*Can I have
   another go?*"
▷ Match the affect of the child or young person
▷ Commentate on behalf of the child or young
   person rather than interrogate
▷ If there is a stand-off, take a step back and use
   the surrender gesture!

Why you'll need to find support for yourself

As a Key Teacher - you can expect
• your own buried unresolved traumas and losses to
   be awakened around these pupils, and to need to
   find some support
• your Key Pupil not to trust you, certainly not at
   first and maybe not for a long time - to them you

are 'just another grown-up'

- your pupil to get mixed up between the past and present, or home and school
- to 'feel' personally attacked because of projection
- to be rejected at times
- to be on an emotional rollercoaster
- to see a spikey profile in your Key Pupil's progress, sometimes even two steps forward, five steps back
- developmental vulnerability
- the long haul

Ways to care for you

Please have a look at (**WAM**) for lots of ideas re: personal and corporate responsibility in attending to the big possibility of secondary stress when working closely with those who have experienced relational stress, trauma and loss.

- Take regular breaks and work reasonable hours. My late friend Rob Versulys (and previous Deputy Headteacher) always used to pay himself back the hours of overtime he worked and I thought this was an extremely helpful suggestion. I have to admit that I haven't adhered to this strategy consistently: but I've been more mindful around my own over-working because of this advice. There will always be more to do, so we may as well take our breaks!

The Key Teacher in School

- Stay refreshed by identifying and attending to your own regulation needs. For example if you feel energised by swimming go swimming regularly (note to self!).
- Stay connected by protecting time with friends and family: connection brings health and well-being.

But for all this discomfort and struggle, those of us who have been doing this work for some time now want to assure you that there can be immense rewards as well, even if they may not become apparent for a long time.

Further professional development for you

Do take up any opportunity to access any training offered, for example the two full days of attachment aware and trauma informed training that is recommended by the Consortium of Emotional Wellbeing in Schools (*see* **Useful Contacts**). We offer this at TouchBase™. Consider becoming an **Attachment Lead** if this is an area that really engages your interest. Check out attachmentleadnetwork.net for more information on how to do this. Read around this subject including **IIH, WAM, TAA, STL** and the rest of the **Attachment Aware School Series**. Check out clips listed at the back of this book to further your understanding.

Key Teacher - EXERCISES

In attachment aware and trauma informed work, it is essential that we are all self-aware. We need to know who we are, what makes us who we are and how we function in the present, so that we can be boundaried in our work alongside troubled pupils. It's important to be aware that being close to these pupils could well re-awaken our own traumas and losses. The process is known as **vicarious trauma** (secondary stress), and it's a reality. If we're not careful there's the risk of merging with the pupil, which would really muddy the water and create some very complex and unhelpful dynamics in the classroom.

So here are some questions to engage your curiosity about yourself. I hope that this brief journey of self-exploration will prepare you to be the best you can be for the pupils whom you support as part of Team Pupil. Try holding your Key Pupil or Pupils in mind as you read through and respond.

EXERCISE I
REFLECTIONS ON YOU
Let's think about you

- How do you describe yourself as a teacher?
- How do others describe you?
- How did you get to where you are now?
- How do others respond to you? Pupils/staff?
- Why do you think they respond in this way?
- How do you think this might influence your work with your Key Pupil?

EXERCISE 2.1

THE REWARDS AND CHALLENGES
OF TEACHING

Let's think about our teaching careers so far

- Why did you choose to be a teacher?
- When do you feel you have had a
  rewarding day at school?
- What rewards are there for you in being
  part of Team Pupil?
- What makes for a difficult day?
- How do you go about maintaining your
  equilibrium on a challenging day?
- How might you integrate what
  you now know about attachment into
  handling challenge?

EXERCISE 2.2
CONTROL AND POWER

Let's think about our experiences of control and power

- Were you parented with authority or control?
- Have you ever experienced fear at the hands of your own parents?
- Back when you were a student, do you remember a teacher exercising too much control and power over you and/or the class? What was that like?
- Do you need to be in control? When?
- What would it be like for you to sometimes follow the lead of the pupil whilst maintaining your boundaries?
- Do you ever feel emotionally threatened in class? When?
- Do you ever feel physically threatened in class? When?
- What support do you need at those times?
- How could you integrate your new awareness into supporting the troubled pupil in your class?

EXERCISE 2.3

ACTING YOUR AGE …

*Let's consider the emotional and social ages of
ourselves and others*

- When would you say you 'act your age'?
- When do you regress? (be honest!)
- How do you feel about yourself when you
  have regressed in some way?
- What do you need at times of
  your own regression?
- How do you handle pupils who are very
  immature in their thinking?
- How do you handle pupils who have very
  immature nervous systems?
- How do you handle pupils who are very
  immature in their actions?
- What sense do you make of why some
  pupils are emotionally and socially much
  younger than their peers?
- How could you integrate this
  understanding into supporting the
  troubled pupil in your class?

EXERCISE 3
THE ROLLERCOASTER OF EMOTIONS!
Let's consider the impact of the journey

- What makes you feel impatient?
- How would we know you were impatient?
- Has anyone ever commented on your impatience?
- Have you ever experienced failure?
- How did you feel? How did you cope?
- What did you need?
- What did you learn?
- Have you ever experienced success? How did you feel? Did you express any feelings around that time?
- Did you share your success with anyone? Why? Or why not? What was that like?
- Was there anything that could have made it better?
- How might your feelings about success and failure affect your work with this pupil?

EXERCISE 4
COMPLETING THE JOURNEY
Let's consider the future

- These pupils often have spikey profiles: so how will you make sense of their regression from time to time?
- What are your hopes for this pupil?
- What are your fears for this pupil?
- How will you inspire and motivate this pupil to become all they were intended to be first time round?
- Create a mantra for yourself to help you keep going when the going gets tough. *When the going gets tough I ...*

EXERCISE 5
RESPECTING OUR BIOLOGY
Let's integrate everything we know

- With all you now know about attachment, what have you noticed about yourself, your friends and family?

- How might you translate what you know about these pupils into good practice with all your pupils?

- If you were truly to respect biology, what would need to change in your personal life?

- If you were to truly respect biology, what would need to change in your classroom? In your staffroom? In your school?

- What first steps could you take to make improvements?

- What support might you need for this?

EXERCISE 6
DEVELOPING PRACTICE
*Let's consider our own developmental journey
and our pupil's*

- Describe how you have changed in your
  practice since starting teaching.
- Who has influenced your practice?
- What has influenced your practice?
- What kind of a teacher do you want to be
  in five years' time?
- Can you think of a pupil who you have
  seen changes in over time? If so, write a
  brief pen picture of them:

  a) *What was their starting point? (their
     background of relational traumas and losses)*

  b) *What were their presenting behaviours?*

  c) *What interventions did you or others put in?*

  d) *What has changed?*

  e) *What next?*

The Key Teacher in School

● Think of a motto you could write for yourself over this next year. Some examples are below ...

Behaviour is communication

Regulate, relate and then reason

Connect before correcting

Connection first

Wonder aloud

Wait, watch, wonder...

EXERCISE 7
BEING A TEAM PLAYER

Let's consider our place in Team Pupil

- Do you prefer to work alone, or as part of a team? Why?
- Have you ever been part of a team that worked well together? What helped this?
- Have you ever been part of a team that went badly wrong? What do you think was behind this?
- How do you feel about being in teams?
- How easy do you find it to delegate?
- How easy do you find it to be delegated to?
- How easy will it be for you to work alongside the Key Adult as equals, but with different roles and responsibilities?
- How easy will you find it for the Key Adult to lead on the pupil whilst you lead on the class?
- How will you manage different perspectives to yours?
- How will you feel about others leading on the discipline of this pupil?
- What do you need to do when times get stressful?
- Who do you need to support you in all this?

EXERCISE 8
RELATIONSHIP CIRCLES

Let's consider who we are connected to and in what order of significance.

Get a large piece of paper and draw three large circles within each other. Write your name in the centre. In each circle, write down those you consider closest to you, working your way out from the centre to those who are more like acquaintances in the largest circle. Then think through who you might put further out than even the third circle, perhaps even in the corners of the page or over the page or those you would not want anywhere on your relationship circles.

Think about what your relationship circles may be showing you.

- How easy was this exercise for you?
- How did you determine what 'closest to you' means for you?
- How connected are you? Do you have a good support network? Or are you quite isolated? Would you like more people in your inner circles?
- If so, how could you put yourself in situations where new connections might be possible?

If you have placed individuals further out on the outer rings or in the corner or over the page, ask yourself how they influence you at this time.

- Are you comfortable with where they are or would you prefer them to be closer?
- If you would prefer more intimacy with them, what will you do to encourage this?
- If you want them to remain at a distance, think about what has formed a barrier in your connection? Has there been any kind of disruption? Is there no way back through to any kind of reunion or repair?

How satisfied are you with your level of connections?

- Do you feel you have all you need?
- If not, what else do you need?
- How can you work towards building further connection?

Remember that all members of Team Pupil need their own Key Adults in order to remain healthy themselves! Interdependency promotes health and wellbeing. If you are going to be part of a support network for a troubled pupil it is essential that you keep your own support network intact and thriving.

- How could you use this new awareness to support the troubled pupil in your care?

B THE DEVELOPMENTAL JOURNEY

By now you'll understand that the Key Pupils we support in class have not experienced the core conditions we all need to develop optimally - the key trio of safety, security and stability. Along with the others in Team Pupil, you'll have recognised your Key Pupil's need for at least one person who can be an attachment figure for them in school, physically and emotionally present, attentive, attuned and responsive most of the time, with some degree of permanency (the Key Adult). You'll know that because your Key Pupil's **attachment system** had not been attended to sufficiently, they are not able to utilise their **exploratory system** - yet - but now things can begin to slowly change. The pupil now has Team Pupil in place alongside them, with you as **Key Teacher**, and in time they will be better able to settle to learn.

So many educational staff have not realised the significance of all this in the learning context. Hopefully now, with some attachment awareness training, you'll have more idea of what is going on and the important role you'll be playing. You'll have a better understanding that behaviour is communication - and of what might be happening for a pupil who is hypervigilant, constantly scanning the room, checking out his or her environment. Or the pupil who is highly anxious, constantly on the move, fidgeting.

There are many pupils who need increased nurture and reduced challenge in all our classrooms. As teachers, we need to *differentiate* for these developmental needs as much as we do for differences in academic ability. Please do bear this in mind in your day-to-day work in school especially in view of the pressures to show attainment that we are all experiencing. The Consortium of Emotional Wellbeing in Schools (*see* p.111) are doing all they can within initial teacher training and with government to raise awareness of the needs of these pupils, so that all stakeholders, including Ofsted inspectors, will realise that it is more important to measure *process* than *outcomes* for these pupils.

By process I mean mapping out the starting point of the pupil in terms of the stress they have lived through to date, the presenting behaviors, the support interventions used, where we are now and the support planned next. Then Ofsted inspectors could evaluate whether the individuals/ school are supporting both inclusion and learning, and can check whether *recovery times after stressors* are reducing or increasing. These pupils will have spikey profiles in terms of their learning outcomes, but the stress they experience should be reducing, together with their recovery times.

So for example, Ryan experienced severe neglect and physical abuse. When he started at the school he couldn't sit in his chair, he would wander around the classroom interfering with others and hurting others and himself. He had regular meltdowns that could last up to three hours. We identified who could be in Team Ryan, and together we worked on making him feel safer through rich, relational interventions such as Theraplay® and PACE. He is now in the classroom most of the time. These days if he gets stressed he uses his Calm Box and he recovers within 10 to 15 minutes! He is now learning and has managed to access Literacy level 2 in the last month.

In this particular support work, we also really need to honour a pupil's developmental pace. Not to do so is disrespectful of the pupil's starting point and the significant impact that **relational trauma** and loss has had on them and their abilities, even on the formation of their brains and their physical aptitudes. And let's also make sure we really respect the kinds of adaptive responses that have served our pupils well in another time and place. The responses we see now were developed in circumstances of overwhelming trauma and hurt, and it's up to us to let the pupil know through our consistent, empathic, attuned care and differentiated approach that school is different and that they can now have the opportunity to develop new responses, in relationship with their Key Adult and Team Pupil.

Rather than increasing and reducing support based on what you think a pupil of 10, 12, 15 or 18 should be able to do at this point, base your support on where the pupil is emotionally and socially right now. There is no fast tracking in development! In fact, if we try and quicken the process, development can sometimes be impeded further! Our pupils don't need further pressure. They need sensitive attuned care. They need us to be gentle with our strength and power as grown-ups. They need us to be *bigger, stronger, wiser* and *kinder* in all our dealings with them (*see* **Circle of Security, Glossary** p.97).

We talk a lot in schools about having high expectations. I would add 'have high expectations within their window of developmental capacity right now.' It is right these pupils need us to dream big dreams on their behalf, and we do. But they don't need us to squash their dreams because we set them tasks and expectations that are forever out of their reach. Sometimes it's too easy to see and hear what we want, expect or hope for rather than what is actually the reality. We need to listen, truly listen,

I've mentioned that these pupils will often have spikey 'profiles' in their progress. Please don't be alarmed - this is part and parcel of the recovery journey. Unlike other pupils, who seem to move upwards and onwards in their learning profiles, these pupils stop and start and regress from time to time. Remember there are a number of stress triggers that can upset and distress the pupil as time goes on. Even if we are fantastic stress regulators as teachers, we simply can't prevent all the possible stressors that occur, including internal ones.

The Key Teacher in School

As I flagged up on p.63, there is often pain involved in acknowledging and respecting another individual's developmental journey. Why do you think it is so difficult for us to stay engaged with someone who is hurting? Because it is painful to see what capacity human beings have to hurt one another so deeply and to accept the developmental vulnerabilities that are the result of relational trauma and loss. Let's be brave and dare to really recognise what is happening, and work together with the resilience factors that our pupils do have, or have developed. The pupils themselves will give you clues as to where they are at and what they need. Let's trust in the human capacity for growth, since, with the right conditions, and so much more awareness amongst staff and carers alike, pupils now have the possibility to thrive.

C THE LEARNING ENVIRONMENT

For these pupils to be effectively supported they are going to need us as teachers to think outside the box, to be creative and flexible in our approach. They will need us to take a few risks in the classroom, experimenting with different ways of working in order to assess the best context for each individual pupil. One size so often does not fit all.

In order to create the right kinds of learning environments for our pupils we all need to notice more. Notice what changes for them when we open that window: when we leave that door closed: when we play music in the background: when we allow pupils to sit wherever makes them most comfortable to do their work ... there is so much to notice (think of lighting, colours and so on, *see* p.32). We can be explicit about what we observe, so that our pupil also has the opportunity to catch up with what is best for him or her. We can also give our pupils gentle challenges to experiment with different contexts themselves. For example, encourage them to have a go at using the beanbag to work in and then check in with them to find out what they prefer. Here are some further ideas of things to think about when you're trying to make the most of the environment to help pupils settle to learn.

Sensory interventions

In class or in a tutor group, you could easily bring up the

subject of stress. Everyone knows what this is. Even some of my youngest clients sadly know what this word means, usually because of their experience. Explain how we all have triggers and that we need to learn to apply the brakes so that our nervous system doesn't get out of hand. Introduce the idea of both sensory and psychological breaks.

Because their nervous systems are so overwrought and dysregulated, our pupils will need us as teachers to increase our sensory interventions to both regulate stress for them and to prepare them for any cognitive tasks we want them to engage in. Sensory interventions basically calm the lower parts of the brain, enabling these pupils to 'think'. Recommendations are as follows (*and for more, please see* **STL**).

CALM BOXES AND CALM PURSES

Calm boxes, purses and bags carry a range of two to three minute activities that have the potential to up-regulate or down-regulate a pupil, usually working in relationship with their Key Adult (*and please see* **IIH**, **WAM** and **STL**). However, I am now encouraging all members of Team Pupil to carry calm purses around with them, to use when they themselves are feeling stressed to a) normalise stress management, as we all have to find ways to manage our stress, and b) to model how and when to use stress relievers. Everyone needs a Calm purse or bag: I have one, and you may well see me using mine before speaking at conferences!

SENSORY BREAKS

These are 10-15 minute activities, usually done by the pupil and their Key Adult outside the classroom. These are usually more intense sensory interventions, using different spaces, larger equipment and can involve food and drink. As **Key Teacher**, your role will be to encourage and facilitate this. Do check in with the pupil on their return and ensure they are not left behind. Use your time to help the pupil get back on track with whatever is going on in the classroom.

SAFE SPACE

This is a minimum of 10-15 minutes of downtime but can be extended as and when necessary, especially when challenge needs to be decreased to support the stabilisation process of a pupil. This downtime takes place in a specially designated space set up with materials that facilitate sensory comfort. This is an especially useful intervention for pupils who run or hide when they move into feeling overwhelmed.

All the above need to be facilitated and experienced together with another person. The ideal person will be the pupil's Key Adult, but you need to ensure that there are enough sensory breaks built into the pupil's timetable, and there may be times when you yourself will need to step in and use one of these strategies together with the pupil. For example, you may know that your particular pupil finds it hard to focus. So you give her a tangle to fiddle with whilst you introduce the lesson. Or you might notice your pupil starting to get agitated in class and so you suggest you both try and balance your whole body weight on your wrists at the table or desk where the pupil is seated.

The use of sensory interventions can also be useful for your whole class. Dr Bruce Perry has stated that if we are to truly respect biology we would regulate a child first by soothing the lower parts of the brain before bringing up a new concept or new learning. He says that this is the best way to optimise the pre-frontal cortex - the thinking part of our brains. It would be fantastic if the whole school community used this research within practice, but until then we must use these interventions for our particularly troubled pupils who are already having great difficulties managing themselves, their alarm systems and their brains.

A further thought is to consider using animals therapeutically within your classroom. Most of the pupils I support love animals and so it makes perfect sense for the school to ensure there is built-in extracurricular time for these pupils to be with and alongside animals in whatever way we can think up. On a personal note, I've just got back from taking my Cockapoo Maisie into a secondary school to run a training session with one of our troubled pupils and her friend. She was so energised by our time together which ended with some rich, relational play: I had encouraged the pupils and the Key Adult to have a kick-about 'piggy in the middle' style with Maisie! Schools using animals this way have noticed a positive shift in attendance and attainment (*check out* Pets as Therapy (*see* **Useful Contacts**) *for more information on how to include pets within schools*). I think probably every school needs a Maisie!

There will be times that an enhanced curriculum will be necessary for a particular child. If this is the case you will need to liaise with the rest of the team in order to ensure the choice of curriculum 'fits' the pupil. Everyone who knows the pupil will need to have a voice and the decisions made will need re-visiting from time to time to allow for the pupil's development.

Do consider timetabling in the use of off-site spaces to engage your Key Pupils as well. In Brighton & Hove we have an allotment project going called Plot 22 which we use as an attachment strengthening project for Key Adults and their pupils. We are also just about to embark on a new project called Therapeutic Forest School. There is so much benefit to be reaped from being outdoors, close to nature. It provides a rich sensory diet and is literally grounding for pupils who have experienced **relational trauma** and loss. Both these projects incorporate Theraplay® and PACE as ways of being and relating (*and see* p.92 re PACE).

Refer to the Senior Manager's book in this Series for more suggestions on creating a calm environment to keep stress levels low in the various spaces in which you teach.

10 pieces of advice from experienced

Brace yourself for possible rejection, but don't take it personally!

There will be frustrating times ahead as these pupils stop and start in their learning and progress, but don't be discouraged. The work is slow but important pathways are being laid down. Stick with it!

Always let the pupil know you have remembered something that they have shared or done. They need to know that they are worth remembering.

If you can't be where you said you would be, or do what you said you would do, say sorry and let this pupil know when they can claim back your time and attention: this means a lot to them. Memory cards seem to really help!

Acknowledge each pupil by name and give them your focused attention, even if you only have a moment. Make it a quality moment. They notice everything.

attachment aware teachers

Take time to identify a pupil's strengths and interests as you then have something to build on.

Don't ever underestimate the power of relationship. I've experienced this myself after thinking Martin couldn't care less whether I was involved or not: he came back to visit me after he'd left secondary, saying that I'd been his favourite teacher. Just goes to show that they do hide a lot of what is really going on!

Say sorry a lot as I've come to realise how much they get mixed up with what you are communicating. You can never be clear enough so just ask for another go. I did and it seemed to generate much respect.

Don't even attempt to win control battles! I've come to realise that these children are experts at self-defence as they have navigated very stressful contexts. Being in control isn't everything, though it can feel that way.

Patience, patience, patience!

D CURRICULUM CONTENT

There are many areas within the school curriculum that regrettably are going to trigger our pupils in terms of memories of loss or trauma. It is easy in a busy school, with a fast turnaround and being under pressure ourselves, to override emotions and just go through the motions of teaching facts and figures in a very neutral, matter-of-fact way. However, there is too much at stake for these pupils for us to operate in that way. The consequences could easily tip class dynamics out of kilter as individual pupils unravel either at the time or later, in response to something they find upsetting or distressing or worse.

So, let's be mindful of how particular topics might be experienced by pupils who are 'wearing' their 'lens' of insecure attachment (*see* **IIH**), and only too aware of their own painful history. Let's also be mindful how many of our pupils will hide their needs and carry on as if everything is fine for them, when really it isn't. Some may even feel trapped in the classroom with no idea of what to do with their big and powerful states, sensations and feelings. Let's feel something on their behalf, and be sensitive.

However, don't then exclude them from taking part. This will only confirm possible feelings of being on the edge, not included and as if they don't belong. Instead give preparation time, time to feel and process in a more private context first, such as at home, with their Key Adult, or in the therapy room. Encourage them to explore the topic to be covered with someone they trust to allow for some expression and processing to take place. Only then should the lesson go ahead with this pupil now ready and prepared emotionally.

For example, when studying the book *Goodnight Mr Tom* (Magorian 2014) which is on the national curriculum in the UK, it would be helpful to first send the book or dramatised version of the book home well in advance to go through together with close, wise adults. The issues of loss raised in this book are often challenging for our Key Pupils.

Or, when covering growth, we usually ask children to bring in their baby pictures, which may be difficult or impossible for children who have been fostered and adopted, and thus deeply distressing. Instead, perhaps we could ask children to bring in a picture that shows growth of different kinds, for example between the ages of four and six, or 10 and 15.

When I recognise that a curriculum area, topic or theme touches a pupil personally, I have found it very helpful to teach the pupil that they have choices about what they do next in terms of whether they open up (or not), and to let others know that. Remember that these pupils have often experienced deep feelings of powerlessness, so it is even more essential that we explain that they now have choices. I often use W.I.S.E Up! - an American tool (*see* **References**) designed to help those adopted internationally, which can also be used in the domestic context at home. The choices (which I have further developed) are:

W WALK AWAY

It is your business. You do not need to say anything. Just keep it to yourself. No-one needs to know that what has happened has affected you at all.

I SAY *"IT'S PRIVATE"*

By saying this you let the other person know that something has affected you, but you are communicating that you don't want to talk about it.

S SHARE SOMETHING

Don't say everything about how it has affected you, but maybe just share one or two aspects.

E EDUCATE

Use the opportunity to educate others. So many people don't understand how relational trauma and loss affect children and young people: so maybe this is your moment.

When using these choices it will be important to help the pupil explore who is in their personal relationship circles and who is trustworthy. These pupils can get very mixed up between selective attachments and indiscriminate ones, trustworthy people and those who cannot be trusted. They will often need our help in distinguishing these different groups of pupils and adults because everything they have experienced can distort their perception and confuse them.

With a young child, you could encourage them to draw pictures of the people in their circles, and with an older pupil they could write names; perhaps it's something the Key Adult in Team Pupil could work on with the pupil (*please see exercise on* p.74).

E THE USE OF PRAISE AND SHAME

Contrary to what we are usually taught in Initial Teacher Training, children who have experienced relational trauma and loss don't function at all well when evaluated, for better or worse. These particular pupils can actually become very dysregulated when a teacher either uses praise or doses of shame within their communication. As teachers, we know why we use (or have used) these techniques; because we want our classes to be socially appropriate. However, problems can be exacerbated using this method with these particular pupils. So instead of using usual behavioral techniques I would strongly recommend that we manage challenging situations using the PACE approach instead, as devised by

The Key Teacher in School

Dr Dan Hughes (2009) (*and see* Attachment Aware versus Behaviourist Approaches chart *on* pp.44-5).

P IS FOR PLAYFULNESS

We have become far too serious in our schools. As one 15-year-old adopted young person said, "*Lighten up! - tell us learning will be fun, not just scary*". Humour serves as a protective factor against further shame, so use basic childlike humour whenever you can, without ever using humour against anyone. Get play back on the curriculum! - as again, we have neglected a great tool for connection. Theraplay® offers a great way of being with pupils in schools. Do check it out and discover how you can use it for individual work, group work and within whole classes at any age! If you use playfulness with the whole class on a regular basis the atmosphere will be more relaxed and this will have a positive impact on everyone.

A IS FOR ACCEPTANCE

Communicate that you accept the pupil at any given moment - whatever they feel, say or do, even if you don't agree with their perspective or understand it. Communicate that their wishes, feelings and beliefs are important and significant. Try not to reassure, problem-solve, distract or ignore. Stay with your uncomfortable feelings for longer than feels comfortable! Let the pupil know you have 'got' or are working to 'get' whatever it is they are trying to say through their behaviour and/ or words.

◖ IS FOR CURIOSITY. CULTIVATE CURIOSITY AT EVERY OPPORTUNITY

Wonder aloud. Guess. Think. Have a go at interpreting what might be going on. Provide some translation. Consider motives and options for motives, rather than immediately judging what you think is happening as fact. You being curious will support others to be curious in your class, and it won't be unusual when you wonder aloud about our troubled pupils.

◻ IS FOR EMPATHY

Many of these pupils do not have very full empathy tanks so use any opportunity you can to fill them up! They need such a lot of tender loving care. Your personal approach will not go unnoticed. They need to know they are not alone. They need to know you are alongside them, as fellow travellers.

I would also encourage you to make connections on these pupil's behalf, to act for a while like the pre-frontal cortex

- their external brain. For example, *"I've noticed that you have a creative part because I have seen you ..."* As their teacher, you'll have lots of opportunity to see this kind of thing, however small; it's a question of remembering it and bringing it up in a sincere way at the right moment.

And when thing do go wrong, at those times of difficulty or conflict, it's important to provide reparative opportunities that you can both engage in, using the word *"Let's ..."* as much as is possible!

Glossary

Additional attachment figure This is the person selected in school to get alongside a child with attachment difficulties, here described as the **Key Adult**. This person could be a teaching/learning assistant or teacher, or mentor. The task is to relate to the child using strategies derived from attachment and developmental principles. Their aim is to create a relationship which will facilitate opportunities for second chance learning, so that the child can have the experience of making healthier attachments than previously. These experiences encourage the development of neural connections in the brain, which in turn leads to the development of conscience, cause-and-effect thinking, logic and empathy.

Attachment history A child's history of significant relationships and the security, or lack of security, safety, or lack of safety, of those relationships with parents, wider family, carers or adopters. It may also include other significant individuals including teachers or even pets. Any type of trauma and loss is especially important to note, even if a loss had been deemed to be in the best interest of the child (for example, loss of contact with an abusive parent): as is any kind of extraordinary stress experienced. We need to know what they have lived through from pregnancy onwards, if there has been any kind of potential disruption to the usual bonding/ attachment process.

The Key Teacher in School

Attachment Lead An Attachment Lead is an appointed
and trained member of staff in the school who seeks to
lead the way in attachment awareness and trauma informed
interventions and embed them into policy on behalf of
troubled pupils. This is usually a member of support staff on
the ground leading through practice with individual pupils, and
a member of Senior Management leading through advocacy
and strategic action amongst the whole school community.
See www.attachmentleadnetwork.net for more information
on the training required.

Attachment system An innate urge within humans (and
other mammals) that impels us to seek promixity to and
relationship with others. Attachment serves two important
functions: a protective function and a secure base effect. It is
in our interest to stay close to another person, especially when
we are very young, defenceless and vulnerable. Staying close
can keep us safe. It is also in our interest to have someone to
act as our **secure base**. If we have a secure base, we are then
freed up to set off out of our comfort zone into the unfamiliar,
the unknown, into unchartered territory - the world is ours
to be curious and learn about. We can do this knowing that
we can return to our secure base before venturing off again.
Our secure base gives us the confidence we need in order to
take the risks required in learning. Our attachment system (of
neural connections and hormone release leading to attachment
seeking behaviour) is activated if we experience anxiety.

Blocked care According to Hughes & Baylin (2012), when a
child or adolescent continually rejects care and nurture from
an adult, the brain systems that support empathy within the
adult begin to close down as a protective response. The adult
can feel frustrated, irritated, hopeless, rejecting or numb. They
may continue to provide care, from a position of 'duty', but find
it difficult or impossible to relate to the child from the loving
and open engaged stance necessary for authentic and healing
relationship (**STL** p.324).

Circle of Security® The Circle of Security® is a relationship based early intervention programme designed to enhance attachment security between parents and children. Decades of university-based research have confirmed that secure children exhibit increased empathy, greater self-esteem, better relationships with parents and peers, enhanced school readiness, and an increased capacity to handle emotions more effectively when compared with children who are not secure. The Circle of Security® intervention and the graphic designed around it are intended to help caregivers increase their awareness of their children's needs and whether their own responses meet those needs. With increased awareness, parents can expand their moment-to-moment parenting choices where needed. In this shift from mind-blindness to seeing what is hidden in plain sight lies the potential to break the stranglehold of problematic attachment patterns, passed from one generation to the next, that can compromise healthy relationships throughout a child's life span. (*With thanks to Jenny Peters and Glen Cooper*)

Containment When a baby is distressed or dysregulated, she needs repeated experiences of her parent or carer being 'bigger, stronger, wiser and kinder' (**Circle of Security®**) to help to 'hold' her feelings and experience and make sense of what is happening, until she is able to do this for herself. Similarly, adult individuals and teams need **Senior Managers** who can create containing environments to support their work containing children who have experienced relational trauma.

Developmental Trauma A term used by Van der Kolk (2014) and many other attachment aware and trauma informed practitioners to describe a child's experiences of repeated or prolonged trauma through neglect, abuse, abandonment, violence, loss, parental substance misuse or addiction. Developmental trauma implies that the child's developing brain will have been impacted, with negative

The Key Teacher in School

effects on the development of their executive functions, motor skills, and capacity to self-regulate, communicate and relate. Left unattended at home and/or in school, the effects of developmental trauma are likely to persist into adulthood and have profound effects on every aspect of the individual's life.

Disrupted relationships/connections Relationships and connections that have been disrupted or compromised for the individual child through having early experiences of loss, abuse, neglect, trauma, domestic violence, or parental substance abuse or mental ill health. Disruption isn't necessarily intentional (although it can be) but can come about due to circumstance: for example, medical complications at birth, having a mother who becomes unwell after birth ... the ordinary development of brain connections may have been disrupted if these experiences happen at certain crucial times, or for prolonged periods. Disruptions often compromise or disrupt trust. There are many children in our care who have experienced intimacy betrayals at the hands of their own birth parents. The deep distrust that has been created out of relational experience is then often projected onto other adults, regardless of their intentions or motives. We can in fact get caught up in their time-warp, experiencing the distress, grief and rage intended for someone else, in another time and place.

Exploratory system An innate urge within humans (and other mammals) that impels us to explore, experiment, play, and thereby learn. The exploratory system (of neural connections and hormone release leading to exploratory behaviour) is activated or reaches its full potential when the attachment system is well attended to. If the attachment system is not attended to, the exploratory system (which is needed for learning) will be impeded by ongoing anxiety.

Fight/flight/freeze response The range of responses we produce in relation to threat or perceived threat. Physiological, emotional and cognitive effects are triggered by the release of stress hormones. Each individual's most likely pattern of response is experience dependent. The pattern can be modified over time.

Hypervigilance A subliminal rapid-reaction mammalian defence developed in response to repeated or continual traumatic experience. The individual becomes wired for a state of high alert at all times to any potential danger in the environment, thus 'primed for threat'. He or she may view or interpret events, words or actions as dangerous which others around them view as innocent or innocuous.

Insecure attachment This indicates a level of insecurity that interferes with the child's ability to relate in a healthy or appropriate way to other people. Such insecurity arose from early uncertainties about the reliability of his or her parent or primary carer. We can observe too much dependence or too much independence in his response to his needs and the satisfaction of those needs. There are traditionally three main types of insecure attachment, sometimes described as avoidant, ambivalent and disorganised.

Reflective dialoguing Reflecting on experience, feelings, thoughts and patterns within a safe relationship with another person, in the interest of receiving support and gentle challenge to make new connections for deeper understanding.

Regulatory system If we have received consistent and sufficient regulatory experiences ourselves, through being attuned to and received by calming and soothing others, especially in our early years, then we are more able to internalise what becomes our own regulatory system (internal and external tools and strategies) to help us self-regulate at times of stress. If, however, we haven't had appropriate

The Key Teacher in School

calming and soothing, at the right time, then our regulatory systems can be over-active and we can end up becoming dysregulated very frequently, even for everyday ordinary stressors. This is why many of our pupils need so much help with regulation.

Relational buffering Rich relational connection serves a protective function. It provides protection from the full impact of stress. It prevents stress from becoming toxic and damaging us. Those who have experienced relational poverty/withdrawal or trauma are very vulnerable and fragile in the midst of everyday ordinary stressors, as well as extraordinary **toxic stress**. This puts them at further risk.

Many of the pupils in our care who have experienced significant **relational trauma** and loss had to manage big overwhelming states, sensations and feelings on their own. Because this occurred when their developing nervous systems were very fragile, they have learned to rely on their feeling brain and primitive limbic system in relation to stressors that come their way.

If we can now stand in the gap and give these pupils the sensitive, attuned care that they didn't have or didn't have enough of in their early years, then we are in effect providing them with the relational buffering they need in order to interrupt the impulsivity that occurs by using the emotional brain in isolation. We can in effect become like 'external brains', lending them our thinking brain to inhibit impulsivity, until they can manage for themselves. Check out the 'handbrain model' on Youtube, by Daniel Siegel.

Relational trauma Trauma experienced by the child on a repeated basis within the context of relationship (often from within early attachments) eg abuse, neglect, violence, intrusion, loss, abandonment and so on. The child may well have experienced overwhelm, powerlessness and terror in the process. The child may well now be completely confused as to the role and purpose of adults, having experienced such overwhelm in their care. It is not surprising therefore that coming into contact with us is going to mean them moving into pseudo-independent states, however caring we may try to be.

Relative dependency This term describes what we may be able to facilitate in schools, in order to give a child who has experienced early relational trauma and loss an opportunity for learning, trust and security through the relationship with a consistent adult who offers sensitive care: in this case, the Key Adult.

Safe space A protected area/space or room full of sensory comfort to support a pupil either to upregulate or downregulate dependent on their state. This space is not used as an area for relational withdrawal or isolation but of time with the Key Adult. There is no expectation there will be talking; the best use of the area is to 'be together'. However both adult and pupil may engage in sensory activites, Theraplay® and PACE. The Key Adult learns the pupil and knows what is needed.

Secondary stress When an individual has experienced profound trauma, those working and living with them are likely to experience stress within their relationships and contact. This stress is a physiological and psychological reality, and those affected will need to seek their own support to help manage it.

Secure attachment This indicates a healthy and appropriate style of relating to other people. An interplay of dependence and independence is observed in response to needs and the satisfaction of those needs, as well as empathy for and generosity towards others.

The Key Teacher in School

Secure base A term used by Sir John Bowlby to describe what a 'significant other' (eg. a parent/carer at home, or a Key Adult in school) can become if he or she provides 'good enough' care for a child. It is from this base that a child can become free to explore and engage with the learning process in school. Equally a room with supportive colleagues can provide a 'secure base' for staff (see **attachment system**).

Social Engagement System Described by Stephen Porges (*please see* (**STL**) p.80) as the open and engaged state achieved when an individual feels safe, and from which the individual will invite communication, understanding and joint interest in the immediate situation with another person.

Splitting When a child presents with a pattern of disorganised and insecure attachment, the adults around him or her may, in response to the strong feelings stirred up by the child's behaviour and responses, become polarised in their view of him or her and each other. Blame and division can easily develop. Team Pupil and the wider system around the child need to find support so that this 'splitting' can be resolved in the interests of the child and of preserving best working practices and relationships.

Toxic stress We all experience ordinary stressors in life. However if a child with a fragile and developing nervous system experiences extraordinary stressors, for example at the hands of his or her own parents, over a period of time, then the child can move into overwhelm. This overwhelm, which can include being flooded with high levels of stress hormones for significant periods, can put undue pressure on the developing body and brain, heart and mind, meaning that their natural development and functioning may become disrupted. This may lead to the state described as 'developmental vulnerability', or trauma.

References

Aspden, K.L. (2015) *Help! I've got an alarm bell going off in my head! How panic, anxiety and stress affect your body* London: Jessica Kingsley Publishers

Belsky, J., Vandell, D.L., Burchinal, M., Clarke-Stewart, K.A., McCartney, K., Owen, M.P. & The NICHD Early Child Care Research Network (2007) Are There Long-Term Effects of Early Child Care? *Child Development* Vol 78, (2) pp.681-701

Bombèr, L.M. (2007) *Inside I'm Hurting: Practical strategies for supporting children with attachment difficulties in schools* London: Worth Publishing

Bombèr, L.M. (2009) Survival of the fittest: teenagers finding their way through the labyrinth of transitions in schools *in,* Perry, A. (Ed.) *Teenagers and Attachment: Helping adolescents engage with life and learning* London: Worth Publishing

Bombèr, L.M. (2011) *What About Me? Inclusive strategies to support pupils with attachment difficulties make it through the school day* London: Worth Publishing

Bombèr, L.M. & Hughes, D. (2013) *Settling to Learn: Why relationships matter in schools* London: Worth Publishing

Bombèr, L.M. (2015) *The Key Adult in School, Attachment Aware School Series Book 1* Duffield, Derbyshire: Worth Publishing

Bombèr, L.M. (2016) *The Senior Manager in School, Attachment Aware School Series Book 2* Duffield, Derbyshire: Worth Publishing

The Key Teacher in School

Bombèr, L.M. **(2016)** *Team Pupil in School, Attachment Aware School Series Book 4* Duffield, Derbyshire: Worth Publishing

Bombèr, L.M. **(2016)** *The Parent and Carer in School, Attachment Aware School Series Book 5* Duffield, Derbyshire: Worth Publishing

Booth, P. & Jernberg, A. (2010) *Theraplay: Helping parents and children build better relationships through attachment based play* New York: John Wiley & Sons

Brown, B. (2012) *Daring Greatly: How the courage to be vulnerable transforms the way we live, love, parent and lead* London: Penguin Books Ltd

Brown, B. (2010) *Ted Talk on Vulnerability* ted.com/talks/brene_brown_on_vulnerability?language=en

Cameron, C., Connelly, G. & Jackson, S. (2015) *Educating Children and Young People in Care* London: Jessica Kingsley

Circle of Security youtube clip youtube.com/watch?v=F6DhnbgRAOo Shark Music vimeo.com/145329119

Clarke, J. & Dawson, C. (1998) *Growing Up Again* Minnesota, USA: Hazelden

Cozolino, L. (2013) *The Social Neuroscience of Education: Optimizing attachment and learning in the classroom* New York: WW Norton

Cozolino, L. (2014) *The Neuroscience of Human Relationships: A practical guide for the inner journey* New York: WW Norton

Forbes, H. (2011) *Overwhelm - Beyond Consequences: Parenting Solutions* Youtube v=X9zLKSoYOaO

Forbes, H. (2012) *Help for Billy: A Beyond Consequences approach to helping challenging children in the classroom* Beyond Consequences Institute, LLC. beyondconsequences.com

Geddes, H. (2006) *Attachment in the Classroom* London: Worth Publishing

Golding, K.S. (2007) *Nurturing Attachments. Supporting children who are fostered or adopted.* London, Jessica Kingsley

Golding, K.S., Fain, J., Frost, A., Mills, C., Worrall, H., Roberts, N., Durant, E. & Templeton, S. (2012) *Observing Children with Attachment Difficulties in School: A tool for identifying and supporting emotional and social difficulties in children* London: Jessica Kingsley

Golding, K.S. & Hughes, D. (2012) *Creating Loving Attachments* London: Jessica Kingsley

Golding, K.S. (2013) *Nurturing Attachments Training Resource. Running parenting groups for adoptive parents and foster or kinship carers.* London, Jessica Kingsley

Golding, K.S. (2014) *Using Stories to Build Bridges with Traumatised Children* London: Jessica Kingsley

Greenhalgh, P. (1994) *Emotional Growth & Learning* London: Routledge

Gregory, A. & Weinstein, R.S. (2004) Connection and Regulation at Home and in School: Predicting growth in achievement for adolescents *Journal of Adolescent Research* July, Vol 19 (4) pp.405-427

Hughes, D. (2004) *Facilitating Developmental Attachment: The road to emotional recovery and behavioural change in foster and adopted children* Maryland, USA: Aronson Inc

Hughes, D. (2009) *Principles of Attachment-Focused Parenting: Effective strategies to care for children* London: WW Norton

Hughes, D. (2013) *8 Keys to Building your Best Relationships* New York: WW Norton

Hughes, D. & Baylin, J. (2012) *Brain-Based Parenting: The neuroscience of caregiving for healthy attachment* New York: WW Norton

Johnstone, M. (2012) *Quiet the Mind* London: Robinson

Magorian, M. (2014) *Goodnight Mr Tom* London: Puffin Classic

Mate, G. (2013) *Attachment and Brain Development* YouTube/v=UbiWLLYSZhc

Music, G. (2011) *Nurturing Natures: Attachment and children's emotional, sociocultural and brain development*

Hove: Psychology Press

Music, G. (2014) *The Good Life: Well-being and the new science of altruism, selfishness and immorality*
Hove, UK: Routledge

Olson, K. (2014) *The Invisible Classroom: Relationships, neuroscience & mindfulness in school* New York: WW Norton

Perry, B. (1999) *Memories of Fear: How the brain stores and retrieves physiologic states, feelings, behaviours and thoughts from traumatic events* Academy version, The Child Trauma Academy Houston, Texas childtrauma.org/wp-content/uploads/2014/12/Memories_of_Fear_Perry.pdf

Perry, B. (2010) *Born for Love: Why empathy is essential and endangered* New York: Harper Collins Publishers

Perry, B. (2014) *Brain Development and Learning*
Columbus Metropolitan Club, Youtube/DXdBFFph2QQ

Powell, B., Cooper, G., Hoffman, K. & Marvin, R. (2013) *The Circle of Security Intervention: Enhancing attachment in early parent-child relationships* New York: Guildford Press

Riley, P. (2011) *Attachment Theory and the Teacher-Student Relationship: A practical guide for teachers, teacher educators and school leaders* Oxon: Routledge

Robinson, K. (2010) *The Element: How finding your passion changes everything* UK: Penguin

Siegel, D. (1999) *The Developing Mind*
New York: The Guildford Press

Siegel, D. & Bryson, T.P. (2012) *The Whole Brain Child: 12 proven strategies to nurture your child's developing mind* London: Robinson

Siegel, D. & Bryson, T.P. (2014) *No-Drama Discipline: The whole brain way to calm the chaos and nurture your child's developing mind* Australia & UK: Scribe

Siegel, D.J. & Bryson, T.P. (2015) *Connect and Redirect Refrigerator Sheet* drdansiegel.com/pdf/Refrigerator%20Sheet--NDD.pdf

Street, K. (2014) *School as a Secure Base: How peaceful teachers*

can create peaceful schools London: Worth Publishing

Sunderland, M. (2006) *The Science of Parenting: Practical guidance on sleep, crying, play and building emotional well-being for life* London: Dorling Kindersley

Sunderland, M. (2015) *Conversations that Matter: Talking with children and teenagers in ways that help* Derbyshire, UK: Worth Publishing

Sunderland, M. (2016) *Best Relationship with your Child* DVD Series childmentalhealthcentre.org/buy-dvds/category

Taransaud, D. (2011) *You Think I'm Evil: Practical strategies for working with aggressive and rebellious adolescents* London: Worth Publishing

Thierry, B. (2015) *Teaching the Child on the Trauma Continuum* Surrey: Grosvenor House Publishing Ltd

Van der Kolk, B. (2014) *The Body Keeps the Score: Brain, mind and body in the healing of trauma* New York, US: Viking

Wetz, J. (2009) *Urban Village Schools: Putting relationships at the heart of secondary school organisation and design* UK: Calouste Gulbenkian Foundation

Wilson, D. & Newton, C. (2006) *Circle of Adults: A team approach to problem solving around challenging behaviour and emotional needs* Nottingham: Inclusive solutions

WiseUp! adoptionsupport.org/store/w-i-s-e-up-powerbook-for-children-in-foster-care

The Key Teacher in School

Useful contacts

Attachment Lead Network	attachmentleadnetwork.net
Attachment Lead Network	attachmentleadnetwork.net
B.A.S.E.® Babywatching UK	base-babywatching-uk.org
Beyond Consequences	beyondconsequences.com
Bruce D. Perry, Psychiatrist	childtrauma.org
Caspari Foundation	caspari.org.uk
Centre for Child Mental Health	childmentalhealthcentre.org
The Centre for Emotional Development	emotionaldevelopment.co.uk
Child Trauma Academy	childtrauma.org
Circle of Security	circleofsecurity.net
Consortium for Emotional Well Being in Schools	jameswetz3@gmail.com

The Key Teacher in School

Daniel A. Hughes, Child Psychologist	danielhughes.org
Dan Siegel, Professor of Psychiatry	drdansiegel.com
Dyadic Development Psychotherapy UK	ddpnetwork.org/uk
Heart Math	heartmath.com
Inclusive Solutions	inclusive-solutions.com
Institute for Arts in Therapy and Education London	artspsychotherapy.org
Institute for Recovery from Childhood Trauma	irct.org.uk
Nurture Group Network	nurturegroups.org
Pets as Therapy	petsastherapy.org
Theraplay®	theraplay.org
Transforming Lives for Good	tlg.org.uk

The Key Teacher in School